CLOUD BY DAY
FIRE BY NIGHT

CLOUD BY DAY
FIRE BY NIGHT

The Religious Life as Passionate Response to God

by

DAVID M. KNIGHT

of the

House of the Lord

DIMENSION BOOKS

Denville, New Jersey 07834

Table of Contents

Part Four

CHARACTERISTICS OF RELIGIOUS LIFE

Preface

Father David Knight's book — *Cloud by Day — Fire by Night* — holds a threefold thrust in its call:

— to an awareness of religious vocation

— to a deeper relationship with God

— to a more radical living out of the three vows.

The title, *Cloud by Day — Fire by Night,* suggests that religious life is a cloud of unintelligibility by the daylight of natural reason, while by "the dark light of faith", the meaning is as clear as strong as a fire burning before one's eyes and within one's heart.

The first four chapters have a textbook format — a feature that bespeaks the author's desire that the volume can be used to teach people the characteristic elements of religious life as well as to foster a deeper relationship with God and a more radical living of the Gospel message.

It is my firm belief that Canadian and American religious who have come to know Father David Knight through his Conferences, Workshops and Retreats will heartily welcome, as I do, this his latest work that is so surely directed to the good of souls and the Glory of God.

Sister JEAN SMITH, C.N.D.

Broaching the Subject

A young girl was walking across a bridge with her fiancé. She was trying to convince him that he was her enough.

"You are enough for me," she said. "I don't care what you earn, or where we live, or who we meet. You are my enough. You are enough to make me happy."

"No," he said, "you might love me enough to marry me, but certainly not enough to be happy just with what I am. I know you love me, but there is no way I can be *enough* for you."

And so it went. Finally the girl stopped in the middle of the bridge and took off the brooch that she was wearing. It was her favorite little thing. When she was sad she wore it to cheer herself up. When she was happy she wore it to celebrate. Now she took it off and simply threw it over the bridge. It dropped into the water and sank out of sight.

"What did you do that for?" the boy asked.

"To show you that I love you," she answered.

"Now that was a crazy thing to do," he said. "I really was not jealous of the brooch. The brooch was no competition. If you had pushed Charlie over the bridge, that might be a consolation to me, but the brooch — that was just a stupid thing to do."

"You don't understand," she said. "If the brooch had been in competition with you, I would have had to get rid of it. And all that would have proved is that I love you *more* than the brooch; that, given a choice between you and the brooch, I would prefer to have you. But that's not what I wanted to say. I wanted to say that you are *enough* for me. If you are enough for me, I don't need anything else. So I threw away the brooch."

"Well why didn't you sell the brooch," he said, "and then we could have made a down payment on the car. That would have made sense."

"No," she said, "you still don't understand. If I had sold the brooch, all that would have proved is that I love you so much that I would rather make you happy by paying for the car than provide myself with the pleasure I get from my brooch. That would be a very beautiful act of love — to prefer your pleasure to my own — but still not the love I am trying to express. What I am trying to say to you, if you can ever understand it, is that *you are my enough.* You are enough for me. And to prove it, the only way I can express it is simply to throw away something I love very much, that *there is no reason to get rid of.* Then you will know that I love you in the way I say: that you are my enough."

She thought a moment and added: "And I will know it too."

A way of saying, "You are my enough" — that is the whole of this book. What follows is going to be dry and intellectual at times, passionate and — hopefully — inspiring at other times. But the story we began with contains it all.

Religious life is simply a way of expressing love. And the love we express is first and foremost love for God, Who alone is man's "enough."

The first four chapters of this book are foundational, and foundations are laid more out of necessity than for pleasure. Those who find them difficult reading might prefer to begin with chapter five. But the first four chapters are the philosophical and theological grounding of all the rest.

In this book we treat the nature and general principles of religious life, celibacy as the key to the vowed life, and community. A second volume will deal with poverty, obedience, spiritual government, and spiritual direction. But this volume establishes already the principles that will be used throughout all the treatment of the vows.

This book has been developing over the past ten years. When I came home from Africa in 1965 for a final year of spiritual formation after four years of theology in France and three years of work as a priest in a bush parish of Chad, I found that the whole scene of religious life had undergone radical changes since I had left the United States. That year was one of the most exciting years of my life. I went on for doctoral studies in spirituality at Catholic University and began giving retreats and workshops to religious, as well as to every other category of people. While writing my dissertation — which sought to get at the reasons for the vowed life, since it was being abandoned by so many at that time — I gathered experience as Acting Rector of the Jesuit novitiate in Grand Coteau, Louisiana; as chaplain to the Religious of the Sacred Heart in the same town, and later as one of the chaplains of Sister's College, Catholic University. I taught spirituality to seminarians for two semesters at Catholic University, continued to give workshops to religious on the vowed life, and became extensively engaged in private spiritual direction and individually directed retreats. After finishing my dissertation I was engaged in a team ministry as pastor of two rural parishes, one black, one white, with the mission to bring about peaceful racial integration. At the same time I taught classes in a girl's academy and in our black parish high school. I went from there to become spiritual director of the Jesuit community at Loyola University, New Orleans, where I also taught a course in spirituality. And from that post I joined the House of the Lord Community staffing this house of prayer in Memphis, which was established by Bishop Dozier. Altogether, during the time this book was developing, I gave over 350 preached and individually directed retreats, days of renewal, and workshops to more than 50 different communities of religious in the United States, Canada, Spain, and Guatemala. During all of this time, and through all of these experiences, the material in this book was being worked out in dialogue and spiritual direction with men and women religious of all kinds, as well as with lay persons in adult religious education courses. Not least helpful were almost five years of regular meetings and discussions with the Jesuit Spirituality Seminar from its beginnings in 1968 until I rotated out of the Seminar in 1973.

It was while giving workshops on the vows for the Canadian Religious Conference of Ontario in 1975 that I felt this book had finally jelled. A day of "poustinia" at Madonna House in Combermere, and two days of hospitality and freedom to write at the house of the Saint Joseph Sisters of Pembroke launched the manuscript. After that my community here at Nazareth House of the Lord in Memphis kept the momentum going by providing me generously with time and encouragement to finish. To all of these people, and to Sister Agnes Stretz of the Poor Clares in Memphis, who typed this manuscript while passing it around to her friends to read and criticize, I am grateful in the Lord.

Now to those who feel, like the girl with the brooch, that in their love for the Lord there is something more they have to express, this book is hopefully dedicated in the Lord.

PART ONE

GENERAL PRINCIPLES

CHAPTER ONE

Of Categories and the Spirit

We don't like the word "categories" today. So let us say a word about categories.

Our purpose in this is not abstraction for abstraction's sake. The real reason for talking about categories is to keep from getting all caught up in them. Categories are tools that help our minds work with reality, and we want to keep them very definitely in their place as tools.

One reason why we are so confused about religious life today is that we can't seem to get a good fit between the categories we have been taught and the reality of religious life as we experience it. The wrench in our hands doesn't seem to fit the nut. Before we start forcing the nut out of shape or throwing our wrench away, let's see if with a variety of wrenches adapted to different angles of the problem we can loosen the whole thing up. Religious life may be one simple reality, but people approach this reality on different levels of understanding; they look at it from different points of view.

For some "religious life" means a complex of sense impressions we are used to receiving when faced with people called religious. If we call a person "Sister" or "Brother" we expect that person to look like something, speak like something, and act like something we are used to. When the Brother or Sister does not look and act the way we expect, we are confused. We hesitate to call this new set of impressions a "religious." We may be pleasantly perplexed or painfully perplexed, depending on whether we like what we see better than what we expected to see. But we are confused.

Phenomenological categories

On this level of what we are used to seeing and hearing, the right category to use is what we might call a "phenomenological category." This just means a shorthand word to describe how a group of people appears to us. A "nun", for example, might mean a long dress, a quiet voice, and a controlled manner. A "Brother" might mean a vigorous enthusiastic teacher in a Catholic school with a penchant for identifying the Kingdom of God with victory over the opposing side in athletic events. Phenomenological categories are what we might call "Hollywood images." They may not come very close to reality as it is, but they come close to reality as people spontaneously and superficially conceive of it.

The most important thing about phenomenological categories is not really the sense impressions they create in us, but the *psychological* reactions they evoke in us. The picture that comes to us through the word "nun" stirs up either good vibrations or bad vibrations, depending on our concrete experience of nuns. That is why it is so important to recognize the existence of phenomenological categories. When someone presents a reality to us under a certain name, we have to know whether we are responding emotionally to that reality as such, as it really is, or just to the associations triggered in us when the name is heard.

In this book we are going to use a lot of names, a lot of terms, that will unavoidably call up a lot of concrete associations from our past experience. These names will evoke images and arouse emotions. If we speak of "religious" and "seculars"; of "clergy" and "laypersons"; of "renunciation" and "involvement" and "separation from the world"; of "poverty" and "obedience" and "religious government" or "superiors", these names will mean to us, on the level of phenomenological categories, whatever they *have meant in the past*. We will hear these names as "baddies" or as "goodies" according to our experience or background. But the whole aim of this book is to get beyond the experience and understanding we have had up to this point; to get beyond and behind the phenomenological associations that go with certain names we give to people and things, and see what reality is meant by these names as such.

Theological categories

This brings us to what we might call "theological categories". These are nothing but some very useful distinctions to help us understand spiritual experience. Theology is defined as "faith seeking understanding" Theology, therefore, follows upon spiritual experience. The Holy Spirit moves people in faith, usually to something they do not fully understand. Later the theologian comes along and tries to clarify, to situate that experience within the overall context of the Church's understanding of herself. By seeing how a new experience, a new movement of the Spirit, fits into what we already know of the Word of God, and into what we have already experienced and reflected upon within our history as the People of God, we come to a clearer understanding of ourselves in the present; a clearer understanding of what we are and of what we are called to be. And since there are many different gifts of the Spirit within the Church, it also helps us to understand ourselves as a whole, and the position of each individual within the whole, if we can come to understand a little better what other people are experiencing, and how their experience differs from and harmonizes with our own. This is the purpose of theological distinctions and categories.

If we are using theological categories, therefore, the word "religious" will apply to a person called and gifted by God to contribute to the People of God in a particular way. And the word "secular" (used in contrast to "religious") will apply to a person called and endowed with grace by God to contribute to the People of God in another way. The distinction between these ways is not something that was created on a drawing board by some speculative theologian and presented to the world to be put into practice. Rather it is something that was created as a reality in action in the lived history of the Church, something people *did* under the inspiration of the Holy Spirit. Christians lived as "religious" and as "seculars" before the words were invented. But as time went on, different people began to reflect on their experience of the Holy Spirit as inspiring their particular manner of living. They did this both to resolve doubts and answer questions that arose within themselves, and also in order to explain their way of life to others who felt inclined to follow them. And so theological categories were born, in a practical effort to render easier and surer the following of each one's particular grace.

Juridical categories

Finally, we can speak of "*juridical* categories". These apply to movements of the Holy Spirit within the Church that have become so clarified by theological reflection that the Church is able to give an official approval to them and know what she is approving. Since the Spirit is constantly prophetic; that is, calling people beyond that understanding of the Word of God they have in the present to deeper insights and to newer ways of expressing that Word in their lives, the People of God find themselves constantly being "surprised by the Spirit." People are faced with some new movement, some new development in the Church, and they do not know, to begin with, whether it is from God, from man, or from the devil. This same anxiety besets the ones who are actually being moved by the Spirit along these new lines. The saints, the prophets, the founders of new movements or communities within the Church were all racked with doubts and fears of illusion. In fact, this fear and doubt is one of the signs of authentic experience of God.[1] And so, when sufficient experience and reflection have taken place for the church's official discerners and spokesmen, the hierarchy, to feel sure they know what is going on, they give approval and reassurance to these new groups and movements by recognizing their contribution to the community of believers in the unity of the faith. In order to give this official approval, the leaders of the Church must know what they are talking about, and define clearly what they are approving. And so a juridical category is born. A juridical category just describes a particular group or movement that the Church understands well enough to define, and sets down the conditions under which her approval is given and will be continued. These conditions, or laws governing a particular category of people in the Church, are

---

[1] Cf. Elmer O'BRIEN, *Varieties of Mystic Experience* (Mentor-Omega, 1965), p. 16, first rule for discerning authentic mystical writing. This principle is illustrated in St. Teresa of Avila's *Life,* chapter 18, parag. 15 (Peers, Image Book edition, 1960, pp. 179-180).

nothing but an expression of the Church's understanding of the direction the Holy Spirit has already taken in these persons' lives. In making such laws the Church is simply being precise about what it is she has discerned so far within this group as being from the Holy Spirit.

Juridical categories are good if they are understood as clarifying and recognizing the movement of the Holy Spirit within the Church so far. They would be bad if they were considered as limiting the movement of the Holy Spirit in the future. Juridical categories simply give approval to certain groups that already exist in the Church; they do not say that no other groups ever will or should exist, or even that existing groups might not evolve in new directions.

When we use such terms, then, as "priest" or "nun" or "layperson", or refer to "religious orders" or "secular institutes" or "religious associations" within the Church, we must know what kind of category we are using. Are we thinking of the *appearance* of these groups of people to us (phenomenological categories)? Or are we aware of their *inner nature* as inspired and endowed with gifts by the Holy Spirit (theological categories)? Or do we simply mean the *existing definitions and laws* through which the Church has given official approval to these groups so far (juridical categories)?

Older communities are renewing

In the Church today — as always, but with a special intensity in particular ages, such as our own — we find two things taking place. The first thing is that the *older,* juridically established groups of people in the Church are struggling to shed the confining, dried skin of the past, to emerge renewed in the freshness of their original life-giving spirit. At the same time they are evolving and adapting to meet the changed realizations and needs of the present. On the level of appearances, neither the clergy, the laity, nor the religious are what they used to be and we should be prepared to readjust our *phenomenological* categories in the light of what is really there. In some cases groups may also be departing, by mistake, from the direction that should authentically be theirs, the direction that corresponds to their inner nature and reality. It is here that *theological* categories can help us discern and judge. We mean this, not in the sense that the Holy Spirit must adapt Himself to the categories of theologians, but in the sense that a theological category, if it is a good one, casts light on the original purpose and direction of the Holy Spirit in calling a group into being, and helps us judge whether further developments are faithful to that original intention. In the midst of all the phenomenological change and theological reflection that is going on today, the Church is adjusting her *juridical* categories just as fast as she can, to give recognition and approval to developments that truly are according to the authentic spirit of a community or calling in the Church. But in the meantime, while the juridical categories are being reformed, much liberty is allowed for experimentation. This allows both good and bad inspiration to find realization and to lead each to its logical results. "By their fruits you shall know them."

New communities are being born

The second thing taking place is the emergence of *new* communities and forms of life in the Church. On the phenomenological level these new beginnings find great freedom, especially in the measure that people do not know exactly what to call them, and so do not have any preconceived model in their minds that they ought to look like, and by conformity with which they can be judged. It may be that these new movements — some of them or all of them — will fall into the basic theological categories that we are familiar with. Perhaps new categories will have to be evolved to situate and explain these new realities in the light of their relationship with the rest of the Church: with her past history and experience; her theological reflection; her diversity of gifts and graces; her sourcebook, the Scriptures. The one error we should avoid is that of making our categories — especially our juridical categories — a Procrustean bed that requires us to lop off or stretch out new realities to fit patterns already established. Categories are to explain reality, not to determine it. Categories are sketches of what already has come to be; not molds into which we must pour everything that is about to become.

Having said this, then, let us pass on to consider that category — and it is a theological one — which is the subject matter of this book. This is the category used to describe and explain that movement of the Holy Spirit which produced within the Church a particular way of life known as "religious life", most commonly identified by the three religious vows of celibate chastity, poverty, and obedience. We will look at the vocation and spirituality of that category of people known in the Church as "religious", or as priests, Brothers, and Sisters who are members of "religious communities".

CHAPTER TWO

Christian Life and Lifestyles in the Church

To speak with any clarity about religious life we must start with a very basic distinction that is found within every Christian spirituality. We can say that the way any given Christian will be called upon to live his life in this world in response to the Gospel will be determined at its root by two fundamental choices: the first concerns the kind of *work* a person chooses and is called to do. The second concerns the *way of life* or lifestyle he will follow:

> Not only, then, is the People of God made up of different peoples but even in its inner structure it is composed of various ranks. This diversity among its members arises either by reason of their duties, as is the case with those who exercise the sacred ministry for the good of their brethren, or by reason of their *situation and way of life*, as is the case with those many who enter the religious state..." (Vatican II, "Constitution on the Church," ch. 2, par 13).

According to work, Christians are basically divided into laypersons and clerics. According to way of life, they are divided into seculars and religious. A priest can be either a secular priest or a religious priest. A layperson can likewise be either a secular (a lay Christian in the world) or a religious (a lay Brother or a Sister). So every Catholic chooses either to remain "in the world" as a secular or to "leave" the world by entering religious life. And in both secular life and religious life there will be the distinction between the lay state and the clerical state, according to the work one is commissioned by the Church to do.

Our topic deals with Christian *ways of life,* and in particular with that way of life which we call "religious life". But just to make clear by contrast what we are and are not speaking of, and to avoid misunderstanding, let us say a word about the options open to Christians in terms of *work.*

Clergy and laity

The basic distinction we deal with here is that between *clerics* (basically priests and deacons) and *laypersons.* According to this distinction people are called by God and the Christian community to one of two permanent, or at least stable, states of life: the clerical state and the lay state. The cleric is called and ordained to a particular function in the Church which is fairly easy to define. It is proclaimed in the rite of Holy Orders and has been extensively studied and taught in connection with the conferring of this sacrament on priests and deacons. With this function go the powers, the dynamism of the Holy Spirit, communicated to the priest or deacon through the laying on of hands. We need not explain this here.

The layperson also is consecrated, by the Sacrament of Baptism, to a triple function in the Church: that of prophet, priest, and king. And with this consecration into the Body and mission of Christ go the powers of Christ that are his in virtue of his Baptism. But the role of the layperson has not been studied, defined, or proclaimed nearly so well as that of the priest or deacon. Consequently most Christians have only the vaguest notion of what it means for a layperson to exercise his prophetic role in the Church, to sanctify the world through his priesthood as a member of the Body of Christ, or to accept the responsibility of stewardship in the Kingdom of God.[1]

Apostolate of the hierarchy — Apostolate of the laity

Another promising field to harvest in would be that of the distinction and interrelation between the *apostolate of the hierarchy* and the *apostolate of the laity.* Here the qualification does not distinguish persons according to permanent or stable *states* of life, but rather according to the kind of apostolic activity they are engaging in, with or without a special consecration to that apostolate subsequent to Baptism. Both laypersons and clerics might engage in the apostolate of the hierarchy. And while all clerics (and also all religious) are by definition committed to the apostolate of the hierarchy, a priest or religious might be allowed or assigned to devote his energies to a field of work that properly belongs to the lay apostolate.

In the briefest of definitions, we can say that the apostolate of the hierarchy is that public and official self-expression of the Church, taken as the whole People of God, which is always mandated by, and subject to the control of, the official leaders and spokesmen of the Church, the hierarchy. This would include the official preaching, teaching, and governing functions in the Church, the sanctifying activity of the Church through the sacraments, and any other work of love and mercy, corporal or spiritual, for which the Church as a whole takes responsibility as for an act of her own public self-expression. For example, Catholic schools and hospitals are part of the Church's public expression of herself. They come under the authority of the hierarchy, and all Catholics

---

[1] See *Supplementary Notes 1* (pp. 225-227) for further clarification of the term "layperson".

who work in them, both laypersons and religious, are participating in the apostolate of the hierarchy.

The apostolate of the laity, on the other hand, is the Christian involvement in this world of a person acting precisely as a Christian, and as a witness to the values of Jesus Christ, but not publicly and officially in the name of the whole People of God as such. An example of this would be a Catholic businessman or politician. The essential task of the Christian layperson in the world is the reform of social structures. The layperson is the leaven of family life, business life, social life, political life. He is the leaven acting within the mass of this world's activity. By its very nature, his apostolate cannot be subject to the practical authority of the hierarchy. He acts as a *ferment* in the life and activity of *this world*. He is not a commissioned instrument of the Church's own official work and activity, as the religious is. The hierarchy must teach him the direction in which the bread of the world must rise. But the layman must decide for himself how to act effectively as its ferment.[2]

The lay apostolate is *private,* in the sense that it is each individual's response — or each individual group's response — of Christian faith, hope, and love to the needs of the world. This response is not subject to the authority of the hierarchy except indirectly, through its need to be in conformity with the general teaching and principles of the Church. Nor does the community of the Church as such, through its leaders, take any responsibility for the judgments, decisions, or actions of individual Christians exercising their redemptive role in the world as lay apostles, according to the light that is within them.

[2] See *Vatican II,* "Pastoral Constitution on the Church in the Modern World," Part I, chapter 4, parag. 43 (Abbott, p. 244).

The apostolate of each individual lay Christian is not mandated in its *particularity* by the Church, although every Christian is mandated very strongly and very positively to the lay apostolate in general; that is, to the task of bearing witness to Christ in every circumstance of life, and working to establish the Kingdom of God in and through every activity and interest of man. The lay apostle is "sent" in the power of Christ to extend His redemption to the whole world; but he is not assigned to any particular task by the community of the Church as such, nor does the Church, through her hierarchical leaders, have any control over the way he carries out the task that is his. Except for his baptismal commitment to be faithful to the general teaching and principles of the Church, the lay apostle is free to apply the Gospel to a particular situation or need according to the light of his own judgment and conscience. In the apostolate of the hierarchy, on the other hand, the Church takes responsibility, and therefore has authority, through her leaders, to assign, remove, or govern individuals in the carrying-out of the missions to which the Church has specifically appointed them.[8]

So far we have spoken of the ways Christians can be distinguished according to the apostolate they engage in; that is, according to the kind of work they are consecrated to do in the Church. It is not within the scope of this book to develop the implications for spirituality that follow from the work or apostolate one is involved in. It should be obvious that there are such implications. Vatican II makes an explicit connection between the work of a priest and his spiritual growth. And everything that is said in the Council documents about the spirituality of the layperson in

[8] See *Supplementary Notes 2* (pp. 227-230) for further clarification of the apostolate of the hierarchy and of the laity.

the world (secular layperson) is tied in with his apostolate as a layperson.[4]

In this book we want to talk about the spirituality of religious, precisely as this spirituality is determined by the *way of life* to which the religious is committed. So let us turn to the distinction between different ways of life in the Church.

Secular life — Religious life

According to the way of life he chooses, and is called to follow, every Christian will be either a *secular* or a *religious*. Within each way of life one might be consecrated either to the work of a cleric or to the work of a lay Christian. In the secular way of life there are both priests (secular priests) and laypersons, just as in religious orders (of men, at least) there are both clerical members and lay members.

A secular Christian is one who is called to live and work within this world, as one who has *invested* in the temporal activities and pursuits of the human race. Secular Christians are a real part of the network of secular professions and occupations. They are "interested parties" in the commerce of human society, because they have bought into this society and cast their own stakes into the economic and political pot. And they live in "the ordinary circumstances of family and social life, from which the very web of their existence is woven."[5]

Religious, on the other hand, have in a very real sense drawn their stakes out of this world. It is true that every Christian has fundamentally and ultimately relocated his treasure in heaven. Baptism is by nature

---

[4] See *Supplementary Notes 3* (pp. 231-233) for the relationship of spirituality to apostolic function and the lifeform.
[5] See *Supplementary Notes 4* (pp. 233-238) for a development of the meaning of secularity.

a preview of Christian death, whereby a person accepts in advance to leave this world and its life and to be caught up in the life of God. But whereas the secular Christian does invest in a very real way in this world while he is living in it, the religious in just as real a way specifically withdraws his investment out of this world even while he is still in it. By the vow of poverty he renounces ownership and no longer has the same personal stake in the economic future of this world that the layperson has, no matter how much he might dedicate himself in his work to struggling for the economic betterment of others. By celibacy he renounces personal, biological investment in the future of the human race, along with the immediate family ties of marriage and parenthood. His bond with his fellow men will be the bond of the Holy Spirit, within the all-encompassing unity of the Body of Christ, but there will be no bond of personal reproduction. Nor will he be "two in one flesh" with any one person except in the unity of the flesh of Christ, where the unity is with all who are reborn in God. And through the vow of obedience he even renounces the immediacy of his relationship with this world in terms of the investment of his time and talents for its development and for his own. He commits the plentitude of his time and forces to the work of whatever mission will be assigned him by the Church within the limits of his community's way of life, whether active or contemplative. And the means he uses for his own growth and development, both in nature and in grace, will be subject to the same authority. The secular Christian is free, and therefore obligated, to respond to the needs of this world in changing circumstances according to the priority assessments of his own discerning judgement for which he alone takes final responsibility. The religious is committed by vow to spend himself according to the priorities of the Church's mission upon earth as determined ultimately through the decisions of his ecclesiastical superiors. The individual religious must take full responsibility for discernment and dialogue with his superiors. But he is committed to leave the responsibility for the final decision in the hands of ecclesiastical authority. Such a commitment implies, and perhaps demands, that the one making it has in a real sense withdrawn his stakes from secular society, *renounced* his claims on society's winnings, and thus is free to contribute to the game played in the city of man on other terms than those of people who belong to the city as such.

Concomitantly, the religious normally does not carry on his life in the "ordinary circumstances of family and social life", but adopts a lifestyle that visibly expresses *separation* from the ordinary way of life followed in his culture. He lives a lifestyle deliberately designed to express a "break" with this world.[6]

Hence it might be theologically more precise, as well as stylistically more balanced, to designate the religious life, in contrast to the secular, as a *fuga-secular* way of life. But we should understand *fuga* here, not according to its usual connotation of "flight" from the world, or of running away; but just in the sense of a breaking-free, an emancipating movement away from certain forms of engagement with this world. Just as there is a kind of physical motion which sets up centrifugal forces within this world, so there is a motion of the Holy Spirit within people which sets up a centrifugal force with regard to the world itself. This force proclaims that the center of man's being has shifted; it is now beyond the sphere of this world, there where man's destiny is centered in the life of the Three Persons of God. And so the fuga-

---

[6] See *Supplementary Notes 5* (pp. 238-242) on religious life as "break" or separation from this world. This topic is also developed in chapter eleven of this book.

secular movement in Christianity is in fact the visible expression of a centripetal motion in the heart of man itself as acted upon by grace toward man's new center: the God of grace revealed in Jesus Christ.[7]

Necessary Christian attitudes toward the world

We should make clear at this point that the contrast between secular and fugasecular Christians is not a contrast on the level of *attitudes* of faith toward this world or the next, but only on the level of the *expression* of those attitudes. All Christians must adhere to the attitudes of radical *acceptance* of and *solidarity* with this world. Likewise all Christians must profess the attitudes of radical *emancipation* from and *transcendence* of this world. In this common faith all Christians are united. But the Christian faith has a built-in tension between the movement of grace (God) incarnating Himself in this world, and the movement of grace (God) drawing man beyond this world into the bosom of the Trinity. The Christian must accept the world and transcend it at the same time; proclaim his solidarity with the world and his emancipation from it in the same breath. He must go toward the world without making it his center, and go beyond the world without rejecting it.

Optional expressions of Christian attitude

These faith-attitudes toward the world are not contradictory; they are complementary to one another. But in the *expression* of these attitudes through lifestyle, man can find himself caught up in *gestures* of expression that *are* contrary to one another. On the level of physical activity, *use of the world* and

---

[7] See *Supplementary Notes 6* (pp. 242-246) for the contrast and complementarity of secular and fugasecular lifestyles in the Church.

renunciation of the world are contraries. So are *separation from the world* and *involvement with the world.* And yet it is not enough to profess Christian attitudes in words; this profession must find expression in actions and lifestyle to be credible. And here we find that by giving expression to one attitude one might seem to deny another. For example, if *everyone* gave expression to the Christian attitude of transcendence of this world by the dramatic gesture of renouncing the world and going to the desert, who would believe that Christians really do accept this world? Withdrawal into the desert is a valid, and even radical expression of transcendence. But if *every* Christian did this — or even every Christian bent on being "perfect" — it would mean that Christianity itself is opposed to use of and involvement with this world. On the other hand, if *all* Christians expressed their acceptance of the world by using and enjoying it, and by deeply involving themselves in the social effort to help other men enjoy it more, who would believe that Christians really believe in anything more than the good life in this world? The Christian ideal would appear as humanitarian and intramundane: an ideal confined within the boundaries of created space and time.

And so we have a real need, within one and the same Church, for *complementary lifestyles,* to really bear witness to the fullness of the Christian attitude toward man and his life in this world. The secular Christian, through his lifestyle, bears witness to God's love for man *in this world* and to the power of grace working to redeem the structures of society and to reestablish all things in Christ even within the *sœculum,* within the time and space of this world. By investing in the world, by putting down roots in the earth through ownership and family, he testifies in action rather than just in words that the world is good and that God wants man to enjoy it, to be at home

in it, and to believe in the power of God in this world
to heal and redeem everything that God has made.

The fugasecular Christian, on the other hand,
bears witness by his way of life to God's love calling
man *beyond this world*. He does this by taking a
stance toward the three basic realities of life on this
earth: things, other people, and himself. By his vows
of poverty, celibacy, and obedience he renounces the
relationship man spontaneously forms with *things*
through ownership, with other *persons* through spousal
love and parenthood, and toward *himself* through independence in the basic choices of life. (Those choices
essentially look to the means he will employ to develop
himself as man and affirm his personality through
contribution to the development of this world). By
taking a stance toward these basic, foundational realities through which a human existence takes root in
this world, he testifies "radically" — on the root-level
— to his faith that the very foundations of human life
have been shifted by the Gospel. The fugasecular
Christian testifies to the reality of man's fulfillment
through grace. By his stance toward this world the
religious expresses in unambiguous terms the reality
of his stance toward the world of grace. By his visible
stance toward things that can be seen, he expresses
his invisible stance toward things that cannot be seen.
This is a stance of faith, hope, and love toward the
transcendent fulfillment and destiny revealed in Jesus
Christ — a destiny which is not from this world and
which cannot be realized through relationships with
this world alone. How the religious vows express such
a stance, and the role such expression plays in the
process of one's growth as a person in grace is the
subject matter of this book.

We repeat that the witness of both ways of life
in the Church is necessary. If all Christians renounced
ownership and marriage, and pulled their stakes out

of this world, then nothing the Church could say about God's love for man's life in this world, or about the goodness of created things, could offset the witness of a unanimous Christian withdrawal from the world. The Christian message would be what it has been lampooned to mean: "Work and pray, live on hay; there'll be pie in the sky when you die." The created, the natural order as such would appear as something irreversibly doomed, something believers should get as far away from as possible, and man's time on this planet would be endowed with no value except as a period of trial and endurance.

On the other hand, if all Christians followed the spontaneous course of marrying and acquiring possessions on earth, and working to build up the city of man — even according to divine specifications — it would be hard for the Church to proclaim with any credibility that Christians really have relocated their treasure in heaven, and are focussing their hearts forward on the Nuptials of the Lamb. The man who is concerned about many pearls cannot proclaim his discovery of the Pearl of Great Price with the same credibility as the man who has thrown all other pearls away. And so, if all Christians dedicated themselves to acquiring, and helping others to acquire, the good life on this earth, Christianity would present itself to the world as just another religion of humanism and esssentially humanistic concerns.

Religious life can only be understood in terms of its complementarity to secular life. The religious presents half the picture of Christian response to this world. The secular person in the world presents the other half. If either half is taken for the whole or viewed outside of its relationship to the other, the picture is distorted.[8]

---

[8] See *Supplementary Note 7* (pp. 246-249) for a commentary on the situation of the secular clergy in our day.

Chapter Three

The Nature of Religious Life: Basic Options

It is the religious vocation precisely as a *way of life* or *lifestyle* that we are considering here. Another topic worth developing, of course, would be the religious life as a vocation to work. In any age, writers and thinkers try to throw their weight to the high side of the boat, to put emphasis where it is needed at the moment. In my opinion, the emphasis that is needed at this moment is on the religious vocation precisely as a way of life or lifestyle. It may be that just a few years ago lifestyle was emphasized in religious communities to the detriment, or even to the destruction of effective work and service in the Church. If so, this was due, not to the emphasis on lifestyle as such, but to the legalism and rigidity that distorted every attempt to live religious life authentically. What concerns us here, then, when we speak of lifestyle, is not a complex of petty little details and fussy observances, but the real heart and soul of religious life, which is the faith-expression of the vows.

To clarify the picture, it will be helpful to recall the familiar division of religious orders into "active", "contemplative", and "mixed" communities. These categories (theological categories) are frequently attributed to St. Thomas Aquinas. How St. Thomas actually divided religious life, and what he meant by his categories, is not the point at issue here. We propose the following distinctions for the purpose of clarifying real options open to us in the present day.[1]

Active Orders

First, there are *active* orders — not active as we use the term today to include all communities that are not purely contemplative and strictly cloistered. By "active" orders we mean single-mindedly active communities, "service organizations". In a single-mindedly active community, some active *work* or task is the whole *raison-d'être* of the community's existence, and the *way of life* is nothing but a means to this end. A religious community founded single-mindedly to run hospitals or schools, for example, would accept — and vow to accept — poverty, celibacy, and obedience as conditions for engaging in the work they were established to perform. The vowed life would be purely a means to the goal of active service that called them into existence. Poverty, for example, would not be chosen as a value in itself. Poverty would mean availability for service to the Church. Should money be lacking, this community would work without salary and live on whatever God might provide. They would not refuse a task because it entailed financial hardship. Should money become abundant, the community would accept it gratefully and live on whatever level of comfort might be available to them — within the limits of Christian simplicity, of course. Obedience would be basically that required within any society that intends to live and work together harmoniously as a family and team. Good decision-making techniques, according to the

[1] For a study of the terms "active", "contemplative," and "mixed" as derived from St. Thomas, see my article "The Active-Contemplative Problem in Religious Life," *Review for Religious*, Vol. 35, No. 4 (July, 1976) pp. 497-516.

best lights of the culture and age, would be imperative. And after that everyone would be expected to subordinate his selfishness, or his personal preferences and judgments, to the overall good and unity of the group, for the sake of the task to be accomplished. Celibacy would be accepted as a sacrifice generously to be mâde for the sake of working more freely for the Kingdom of God. Where husband, wife, or family would limit one's availability for the task to which the community is committed, every member would willingly and generously sacrifice marriage in order to be more available to God. In short, in a singlemindedly active community the whole purpose of the community's existence is the work to be done, and everything else is designed to be a means to this end.

Contemplative Orders

In singlemindedly *contemplative* orders, the *way of life* is the community's whole *raison-d'être* and *work* is nothing but a means to be free to live the lifestyle that is according to one's interior call. The singleminded contemplative goes out to the desert, or into the monastery, in order to live in a certain way. He works to support himself, or to find some relaxation or distraction from the intensity of his prayer. But what he accomplishes through work is not really a goal in his life. For him poverty, celibacy, and obedience are goals in themselves — not in the sense that they are ultimates (only love is an ultimate in Christian spirituality), but in the sense that they constitute the very form of his life, and where they exist according to their true nature, his life will tend to be what it should be. (As we will see later, I understand prayer, and a life of prayer, to be implicit in the vow of celibacy, where celibacy is lived according to its true nature). For the contemplative the prayerful life of the vows is an "end" in the way that health is an end

for the body. Health is subordinate to being, to life.
But health is the well-being of the body. Likewise
the vows are subordinate to loving, to being-for-God.
But to live the vows authentically is to live out in
reality the expression and fact of one's love for God.
Hence, for a contemplative community, living the
vowed life prayer-fully is the whole immediate purpose
of the community, and everything else is a means to
this end.

"Mixed" Orders

In *mixed* religious communities, which means
mixed active-contemplative, the community exists for
the sake of two things, neither of which is just a
means to the other. A mixed community comes together both for the sake of living in a particular way,
the way of the vows, and for the sake of doing an
active work in the Church. Each of these goals is
accepted for its own intrinsic value; neither can be
reduced to being just a means to the other. This
means that in a mixed community it is not the
demands or circumstances of a task to be accomplished
that determine whether or in what degree the community will be actually poor. Poor is what the community has chosen to be regardless of whether the
work demands it or even benefits from it in any immediate or verifiable way. Obedience, too, is chosen,
not just for the sake of efficiency, coordination, or
intramural peace, but for the sake of an objective
surrender to Christ through His Church, a surrender
that reaches the personal depths of one's existence.
And celibacy is chosen positively for itself, for the sake
of what it expresses and realizes in terms of one's
relationship with Christ. It is not just accepted as a
condition required for the accomplishment of a task.

In mixed communities work, too, is chosen as a
goal that is worthwhile in itself, and not just as a

contribution to the way of life. The active work of a religious should contribute to his growth and fulfillment, both in nature and in grace. But the work is chosen and engaged in, not simply with the individual's fulfillment in mind, but for the sake of helping others, for the good to be accomplished in the Kingdom of God through that work itself. Hence, in a mixed community one does not select or measure the work one will do just by the criterion of what promises to be most developmental for oneself. It is understood, of course, that in the whole picture of things any work one does in response to the will of God and the needs of others will be developmental for the person doing it, no matter how much sacrifice of personal goals it may seem to entail at the moment. It is also understood that to ignore personal goals by a purely task-oriented assigning of persons to functions is ultimately to lose sight of the Kingdom of God.

In this book the problem that concerns us most is that of the "mixed" religious communities. What we say about the vows will be applicable to contemplatives also, of course. But it is the mixed communities — the ones we are accustomed to refer to indiscriminately in popular language as "active religious" — who are most in need of re-accenting the value of the vows. What I fear is taking place, and it is a fear echoed to me by many other religious, both men and women, from a cross-section of religious communities, is that many active religious orders, founded to be "mixed" active-contemplative communities, have in fact become, almost without noticing it, "purely active" or singlemindedly active communities: "service organizations". More and more religious are awakening with distress to the realization that what really determines their lifestyle is not any theory or faith-vision of the vows as such, but simply the demands and the benefits of active, professional work. The material standard of living in a given religious house is pegged pretty closely to the income of the institution or parish served, or to the success of the community's begging program. In affluent areas religious live well. In poor areas they might live a little less well, but if they are supported by an outside source of income, they probably live on a significantly higher scale than the people they serve. The level of obedience is almost in indirect proportion to the professional status of the individual or community. And prayer, whether individual or communal, stands in line for the moments left over, if there are any, after the demands of work have been satisfied. These are broad generalizations, of course, but they are indications of a reality that is only too familiar in its details to too many religious. Individuals are turning to houses of prayer, or looking at contemplative life, in an effort to recapture something of the depth and style of life they hunger for. It is obvious that within the hearts of active religious there is a yearning that is not being satisfied. It is my belief that what is missing is a style of life that is an integral, an essential element of their calling; a way of living that puts religious into contact with the contemplative, the faith-dimension of their vocation. It is this way of living that concerns us here.

CHAPTER FOUR

Way of Life — Way of Growth

The constant theme of this book is going to be that the vowed life is a way of personal, spiritual growth through being a way of graced *self-expression*. We grow in grace by letting *grace express itself in and through our natures*. We grow in that faith, that hope, that love which we express in action in our lives.

A second thesis of this book is that the most positive element of the vowed life is *renunciation as such*. It is precisely the renunciatory aspect of the vows which makes them radically and unambiguously expressive of Christian faith, hope, and love. And since, in living the vows, it is precisely through the *self-expression of the grace that is within us that we grow*, this leads us to the paradoxical conclusion that it is in fact the most negative aspect of the vows — namely their renunciatory content — that is the most positive thing about them.[1]

All of this requires some explaining, and the basic explanation can be reduced to three principles.[2]

---

[1] See *Supplementary Note 8,* "Renunciation as a concept" (pp. 249-268) for the positive meaning of Christian renunciation in our day.

[2] These principles are all gleaned from Karl RAHNER, S.J. See his *Spirit in the World* (Herder, 1968), pp. 67-77, and *Hearers of the Word* (Herder, 1969), pp. 36-44; *Theological Investigations IV* (Helicon, 1966), pp. 221-252; and Otto Muck, *The Transcendental Method* (Herder, 1968), pp. 181-204. They are most clearly presented, however, in my dissertation: *The*

*The relationship between
personal growth and awareness*

The first principle concerns the *relationship between personal growth and awareness*. It can be stated this way: We *are,* as persons, in the measure that we are *aware* of ourselves as having and exercising freedom, and as creating ourselves as persons through this exercise of freedom.

What does it mean to be "fully a person" as we use these terms today? In the time of St. Thomas Aquinas, a "person" just meant any being endowed with intellect and will, and you wouldn't speak of "becoming" a person as we do today. But in our ordinary usage of the word — which reflects some insight into reality, no matter how vaguely recognized it might be — we employ "person" as a term admitting of degrees. One can be "more" or "less" of a person; one can "become" more of a person than one was before.

When we speak like this, we are really speaking about the recognition a person has of his *freedom,* and about the responsible use he makes of it. The man who is completely culturally conditioned, for example, is hardly a "person" yet, because he is not even aware of what it means to choose. He accepts everything as he has been conditioned to accept it; he is not really conscious that there are options. For him there is only one "real" way — that is, only one way worth considering — to eat, to dress, to select a house, to choose one's friends, or to elect one's form of government (assuming governments should be elected). He has never really seen another way of life

Implications for Spiritual Theology of Karl Rahner's Theology of Renunciation Studied in the Light of His Concept of Man. Catholic University of America, 1970.

as a possible option for himself. And so he has never become conscious of really *choosing* the kind of life he leads. It is only when he becomes aware of himself as personally adopting his attitudes and values, and as *having options and choices* to make that he discovers what it means to be free.

A second factor in becoming a person is to realize that man *creates himself* by the choices he makes. God creates man as a human nature; man creates himself (in cooperation with God) as a person. In response to the question, "*What* are you?" we answer, "A human being; a woman, a man." In response to the question, "*Who* are you?" we give our name. But a name by itself is a nonsense syllable. That is why it is so hard to remember names until we have some real knowledge of the persons to whom they are connected. A name has no content except the history of one's having-lived. What a person's name really means, what it will mean when it is written on his tombstone, is the cumulative effect of all the free responses that person has made to life: to things, to other persons, and to God. And so it is crucial for us to realize that when we make a choice we are "writing our names" — we are creating ourselves as the persons we will be for all eternity. Not to realize this is to fail to enter into full possession of ourselves as we really are. It is to fail to understand the potential and power of our freedom. It is to be not yet a person.

On the level of personhood, then, we can say that to *be* and to be *aware* are the same thing. We *become* persons in the measure we become aware of what it means to be one.

Of course, it is always possible for a man to back off from being a person, once he has glimpsed what personhood entails. Freedom can be terrifying as well as enticing. Those who back off from the experience will never really be aware of what it is; only of what it could be. They will remain on the level of would-be persons.[3]

Awareness and growth in grace

Can we convert what we have just said into a principle of growing in grace? What does it mean to "grow" in grace? Grace is not a quantity that can "increase". It is not like a muscle, which grows through exercise. Grace is nothing but the reality of God dwelling with man, uniting Himself to man on the level of being. And here we have the key. In the union of grace God joins Himself to man *on the level of being, prior to operation.* This is the only such union that exists: only with God is it possible. Only God can unite Himself with another on this level. Creatures can only join themselves to each other through the medium of operations: one speaks, another listens, and some union of minds is achieved. One sings tenor, another bass, and a blended result is attained. These are the results of two operations, each proceeding from a different agent. But when God joins Himself to a human being in grace, one and the same operation proceeds from both God and man, each one the personal agent of the single, unique operation. A graced operation is not a blend of God's operating and man's; it is one and the same operation proceeding from God and man, each one the personal agent of the operation. And so a graced operation is fully human and fully divine. The whole operation, and not just part of it, belongs to man; the whole

[3] See John C. HAUGHEY, S.J., *Should Anyone Say Forever? On making, breaking, and keeping commitments,* New York (Doubleday & Co.) 1975, esp. pp. 17-36. See also Erich FROMM, *Escape from Freedom,* New York (Holt, Rinehart, & Winston), 1941.

operation belongs to God. It is God's action; it is man's action, without division.

What we are talking about here is a union on the level of *persons*. God and man are united on that level where an act of personal self-expression begins. A graced operation is man's act as person; it is God's act as Person. For example, you are walking down the hall and you meet a friend. The one you meet seems depressed. God within your heart says to you (without any identifying call number!), "Let's smile at that person." You feel the inclination to smile (it is already your own inclination) and you either follow it out or you do not. If you do not, recalling that you smiled at this same person yesterday and were snubbed, the movement of grace is aborted. But if you do smile, the smile that comes out — and the act of love it expresses — is literally human and divine. It is God's personal act of self-expression. It is your personal act of self-expression. You and God are united on the level of person, expressing one and the same act of love in one, unique operation of smiling that belongs fully to you both.

Now, to "grow in grace" obviously means to grow into deeper and deeper union with God on this personal level. It means that man becomes more and more sensitive to the inspirations of God in his heart, less and less resistant to those inspirations. It means that the choosing "self" man identifies with will be less and less his isolated, human self; more and more his self as joined to God. He will say now, with St. Paul, "I live now, not I, but Christ lives in me." Only he will experience this, not as the loss of himself, but as the discovery and realization of his true self in Christ. In perfect union it is not Christ as the "other" who asks or inspires, but the voice of Christ has become the voice of man's own heart surrendered to Him.

Obviously this kind of union is not accomplished overnight. Sometimes man will experience the inertia of his nature, of his human drives and passions, fighting against the "law of his mind", against the truth and values he has embraced as person and with which he has identified his true self. At other times man will experience God as being very much the "other", as demanding, even ruthlessly, what seems to be the annihilation of himself. But the more man becomes *aware* of the Voice that speaks within him, offering him new options, inviting him to unexpected choices, calling him to deeper identification with the One who is speaking, and the more man identifies, freely and confidently, this Voice as being his own Way, his own Truth, his own Life, the more he will have grown in grace. Thus, to þe *aware* of oneself as having new options as a graced person, and as creating one's true, one's own authentic self as a person-in-grace precisely by responding to those options, is what it means to authentically *be* in grace.

Of course, just as it is possible to back off from freedom and fail to be a person, so is it possible to back off from surrender to God and fail to be brought into deeper union with Him. But if we back off from surrender to God, we will never really be aware of what the options are He holds out to us, or of what it is to find one's true self by losing oneself in Him.

Real-symbolic expression

Our second principle deals with *self-realization by means of real-symbolic expression*. This means that we realize ourselves as persons — in both senses of this word, as discovering and as making real — by *expressing* ourselves externally in actions. These actions are called *symbols* because they are the visible, external expression of the invisible, interior choices

of our hearts. They are called *real*-symbols because
the "stuff" of the expression is not just words but an
investment of our being. The gesture that symbolizes,
that expresses our hearts is not "just" a gesture, "just"
a symbol; it is a symbolic gesture that *makes real*
what it expresses, like the gesture of giving one's life
for one's friend. It is a word spoken in the language
of reality, a word of decision spoken in flesh and
blood that engages and involves our being. A real-
symbolic gesture is made when we express ourselves
through the disposition of something real and valuable
to us: our possessions, our time, our lives. A real-
symbolic gesture is a word made flesh in action.

Through real-symbolic gestures we *discover* the
truth of our free choices. Until a man has expressed
his choice in action, and in some action of propor-
tionate consequence to himself, he does not know
whether he has really chosen, or whether he just
thinks he has. The old Quaker said to his minister:
"I sure felt sorry for that man." The minister re-
sponded: "Yes, friend; but did thee feel in the right
place — in thy pocket?" A man doesn't know whether
he loves his fellow men, or his ideals, enough to die
for them until he actually risks his life. That is his
"moment of truth".

In real-symbolic gestures, then, we both *discover*
"who we really are" — we become *aware* of the
person, the freedom-event that we are — and we *make
real* the person we have chosen to be, the orientation
of ourselves that we have decided on. To *do* something for one's fellow man in love is both to discover
that one loves, and to make that love real.

The Transcendental Method

Our third principle involves the use of real-symbolic expression in order to *realize one's relationship*

with the transcendent; that is, with God. It makes use of the "transcendental method" — which, stated simply, is this: In order to realize my relationship with the Transcendent Object (God), Who by definition is not an object of human operation, because He is beyond the range of every human operation, I establish a relationship with *objects in this world* which is such that it requires as the *condition for its possibility* or intelligibility the reality of my relationship with God. Put more simply this means that I act toward things or people in this world in a way that does not make sense without God. Then I know that my relationship with God is real, or that God is "real" to me, because the reality of my action in this world does not make sense without Him. I know that I am "taking Him for real".

The use of the "transcendental method" as we have explained it here does not establish the fact that God is real; just that He is real *to me.* It serves as evidence to me that I am really *responding* to Him in faith, hope, and love. The method can also be used to demonstrate the fact of God's existence, but that is not a question that concerns us here.

We do not pretend that anyone can ever know with infallible certainty that he is responding in a graced way to God. But in the measure that a man can have moral certitude about the real motivation of his choices, he can know that this or that deliberate stance he has taken toward the world simply would not be intelligible in his own life except as a response of faith to the revelation of Jesus Christ. Hence, the transcendental method as we use it here simply means that a man *realizes* his relationship of faith, hope, and love toward Jesus Christ by *expressing* himself in this world in external, real-symbolic actions which are such that they simply do not make sense except as responses to the Gospel.

If we put all of these principles together, we come up with a general principle for growing in grace: *we grow in grace by letting grace express itself radically and unambiguously in and through our natures.* We grow in faith by letting the faith express itself in our lives. We grow in hope by letting hope appear in our actions. We grow in love by expressing love in concrete ways that involve the investment of our being. The more *radical* these acts of self-expression are — that is, the more they reach down to and engage the very roots of our being — and the more *unambiguously* they proceed from pure faith, hope, and love, the more productive they are of growth.

Application of these principles to prayer

For example, suppose I begin to wonder whether the Person of Jesus Christ is really "real" to me. I wonder if I really believe that one can grow — or that I myself can grow — in personal knowledge and love of Christ *as a person,* in this life. I wonder if I really do know Him as a person, or if I really want to.

Suppose then I begin to pray — not just on an occasional basis, when something moves me to it, but on a daily basis, out of commitment. Let us suppose that I begin to *invest* a significant amount of my time each day (and my time is my life: that is all life is, the time between birth and death) in doing *nothing but* seeking to know Christ better through prayer. I reflect on the Gospels, I meditate, I contemplate, I just remain silent in the presence of God, waiting. Let us go further and suppose that my prayer seems to be useless. I get no good thoughts, I get no good feelings. I have no mystical experiences. I do not even feel that I am in the presence of Anyone.

I know that Christ is real to me.

I know it because I am taking Him for real. I am taking a stance toward everything else in this world, for a significant period of time each day, that could have no other purpose, meaning, or foundation than faith in the fact that Christ can be known as a person. For a significant amount of time each day I invest my time, my being — in doing what? In doing *nothing but* seeking the face of God. The "nothing-but-ness" of my prayer is important. It is that which makes it unambiguous. It is when my prayer can be *nothing but* the expression of my faith that God will let Himself be known, when it is nothing but the real expression of my desire to know Him, that I discover through my prayer the reality of my faith and love for Him. It is then that I know He is real to me.

There is an old, standard joke about the Jesuit and the Dominican who were walking in the garden during meditation. The Jesuit was smoking, the Dominican was not. The Dominican said to the Jesuit, "Father, I asked permission to smoke during my meditation and it was denied. How did you get permission?" The Jesuit answered, "I asked permission to meditate while I smoked."

I used to think this was a joke. Now I see it as an important observation about prayer. It is good to pray always — when one smokes, goes for a walk, while listening to music, talking to one's friends, etc. But these are moments when my prayer, considered as an act of self-expression, an act expressive of my own faith, hope, and love, is ambiguous. If I go out for a walk and a smoke, then what my action immediately expresses is a desire to take a walk and have a smoke. If at the same time I lift up my thoughts to God and love Him, so much the better. That is to pray while I smoke. But there must be other moments — and especially during those periods of my life when I find it most difficult to lift up my thoughts to God or to keep them there, and most hard to believe that I love Him — when I must express my faith and love in an action that can have no other meaning or explanation except as the expression of faith and love toward Jesus Christ. That is when I "go into my room and close the door and pray to my Father in secret." When I go to pray like that I do not smoke.

This is the special value of arid prayer. When I get no satisfaction out of meditating, then I know I am not just investing my time for the human satisfaction of getting good thoughts or insights. When I get no feelings of devotion or peace during prayer, and my good resolutions either just don't get made or never seem to pan out, then I know I am not just investing my time in some kind of technique for self-perfection. (This is one of the distinctions between Christian mental prayer and various psychological methods for achieving inner tranquillity and relaxation, such as Transcendental Meditation, popular Yoga, and the like). The more arid my prayer, the more unambiguous it is as an expression of pure faith, hope, and love toward God. We need to know this. When prayer is consoling it doesn't cause us any problems (at least, none we are conscious of). But when prayer is desolate we think we are doing it badly. It may be that just the opposite is true.

The essential of prayer is that it be a real expression of faith, hope, and love. The faith my prayer expresses is the faith I will grow in. If, for example, I go to pray for God's help before an examination, I grow through that prayer in the faith I express in God's providence and power. If I go to pray because I have sinned, I grow in the faith I express in God's love and forgiveness.

What if the faith I want to grow in is precisely that core mystery of the Christian revelation that now,

through the Incarnation of Jesus Christ, the out-
pouring of the Holy Spirit, and the indwelling of the
Trinity in our hearts, God has become so near to
man's mind and heart and will that man can *know*
Him as a person, and *grow* in this knowledge, and in
the love that accompanies it, until he arrives at perfect
union of mind, and will, and heart with God? What
kind of prayer will express precisely this faith that
God can be known and loved as a Friend?

I think the only prayer that expresses this is *committed* prayer. This is because a commitment to seek
the face of God day after day can have no other
motive than belief that God can be better known, and
a desire to draw closer to Him. (We are speaking here
of mental prayer — meditation or contemplation —
because one might also commit oneself just to singing
the praises of God every day in prayer, and that commitment would express another act of faith: the conviction that God is good and worthy to be praised at
all times, worthy even of the dedication of one's whole
life just to singing His praise).

The very *fact* of committing a significant amount
of time each day to mental prayer is a radical and
unambiguous expression of belief that Jesus Christ
can be better known and loved, and that it is worth
a significant investment of one's life-time to grow in
friendship with Him. (How much time is "significant"
depends on the circumstances of one's life. For a
monk in the desert half an hour a day would hardly
be significant. For an extremely busy person it might
be).

Prayer as we describe it here is a real-symbolic
act. It is an external expression of an interior response. It is a real expression, a word-made-flesh in
action, in the investment of our being, our time. It
is a stance taken toward the created reality of this
world: in prayer we turn away for a moment from

all that is created to face the uncreated reality of God.
Or we seek the reality of God incarnate in the humanity of Jesus Christ. In this stance toward all that
is created, in the solitude of our prayer, we realize
the stance of our hearts toward God: we discover it
in the act of making it real. And so we grow in
awareness of who God is to us, and of who we choose
to be for Him. We grow in an affirming awareness,
in conscious choice. We accept and affirm the re-
creation of our persons by grace as responders to the
Word of God.

Prayer, on the level we are talking about, is an
act — so long as it endures — of total separation
from the world, of withdrawal into solitude. But in
that solitude we rediscover the world. By affirming
our relationship with God, we reaffirm our relationship with the world, this time in the authenticity of
God's terms, not in the selfishness or deceptiveness of
our own. Prayer is an effective renunciation of the
world for the brief moment that prayer lasts; but it
is an affective embracing of the world forever.

We see here that what is really most expressive,
most unambiguous, most positive and growth-pro-
ducing in our prayer is precisely its *renunciatory
aspect*. Prayer is unambiguously attention to God in
the measure that it is attention withdrawn from everything else. I know that I am seeking the face of God
in prayer when I know that in what I am doing I
cannot possibly be seeking anything else. This does
not mean that as a practical method we should necessarily attempt to empty our minds of all concepts and
images of created things, or to think of nothing but
the pure spiritual reality of God. It just means that
we withdraw, we separate ourselves physically from
the world first of all by going into our room, our
solitude, and closing the door. And there we "pray
to our Father in secret" by renouncing any activity

that is not unambiguously a centering of our thoughts and our desires on Him. We might center our thoughts and desires on Him through the humanity of His Son, or that of His Son's Mystical Body on earth, or through anything else that reveals Him. The only rule here is that, for our prayer to be an unambiguous expression and experience of our faith, hope, and love, it must not be an activity that makes sense as anything else. In the beginning it will usually be a mixture of many things. But usually, if we persevere in a life of prayer, God will insure the unambiguity of our prayer by drawing us into the dark night of faith.

We have spent a long time illustrating the principles of spiritual growth through this one example of prayer. This is appropriate, because prayer is the heart and soul of the vowed life. It is also very practical to have done this, because the principles we have just explained are the foundation and support of everything we are going to say about the vows. It is important, then, to understand them.

PART TWO

CELIBACY

Chapter Five

Celibacy as Self-Expression

In our treatment of the vows self-expression will be the key to the meaning of each one. Each vow is a real-symbolic gesture of faith, hope, and love through which a person takes a real and visible stance toward one of the radical (root) values of human life on this earth, toward one of the basic realities of human existence. Since the stance taken is one that **does** not make sense except through faith in the Gospel, the person both *expresses and experiences* through this stance toward created reality the depth and reality of his stance toward the transcendent God who has revealed Himself in the Gospel. The vows, therefore, are a means of self-realization in grace through the expression and experience of one's supernatural faith, hope, and love. And we use the word "self-realization" here in both of its senses: as *discovering* the truth, the reality of one's personal, free self-orientation in response to grace; and as making that free response, that act of graced self-creation real.

We will use celibacy in this treatment as a key to the vows. This choice does not impose itself: poverty or obedience could also serve as starting points. But we choose to use celibacy as the key because of the kind of relationship with Christ that it brings before our eyes.

The expression of faith

What celibacy expresses is real belief that it is possible to have with the person of Jesus Christ a relationship of growing intimacy and love during this life. Celibacy is a way of affirming that true *friendship* with Christ is possible on this earth — friendship as real, as satisfying, and as developmental as the deepest relationship of human love between persons is capable of being.

Real-symbolic gesture

How does celibacy express this? The vow of celibacy is a real-symbolic gesture. That is, it is a way of giving expression to one's belief through actions that engage one's being. The vow of celibacy engages one's being in two ways: first, it is a renunciation of marriage — of spousal love — with any and every human partner on earth. Secondly, it is a positive commitment to some concrete, specific things that express and embody a relationship of spousal love with Christ.

Awareness and self-realization

By the renunciation of marriage the celibate "realizes" — that is, he both discovers the truth of and makes actual the reality of — his faith that an equivalent (not to say surpassing) relationship of love with Jesus Christ is possible. Rahner says, speaking of the eschatological expression of the vows, that a person cannot really know that he believes in the two birds in the bush until he lets go of the one bird in the hand.[1] We can say in the same way of celibacy:

---

[1] Karl RAHNER, "On the Evangelical Counsels," *Theological Investigations VIII*, (Herder, 1971), p. 155.

You don't really know that you believe in the relationship of love that is possible with the invisible God in your heart until you give up the visible girl (or man) in your arms.

> The value of celibacy consists in this, that it is a means to existential realization of the place Christ holds in one's life — and therefore it is a means to making that relationship with Christ a consciously-possessed, effective reality. It is a means to union with Christ because it is an act of unequivocal gift of oneself to Christ (unequivocal on the presumption of psychological normalcy and sufficiently informed spiritual theology). It is an experience of faith, because it is an act which, in its context, faith alone can justify. In many celibates' lives marriage might even augment or at least facilitate service. But celibacy is not chosen for the pragmatic aspects of service only; it is chosen in order to help the person "realize" better (in both senses, of discovering and of making real) the relationship he has through grace with Jesus Christ and with the Body of Christ, and thereby to make that person able to serve the Church simply by *being* what he is, a witness to the light that is within him. Celibacy is a form of that mysticism which we define as an awareness of oneself in relation to God, or of oneself as responding to God. It is a deep and unequivocal experience of taking God at His word.[2]

Celibacy is an act of taking Christ for real through existential risk. That is what makes our faith in Christ real — both as actualization and as awareness.

Celibacy not for the sake of work

Celibacy is the entrance into a specific relationship with the person of Jesus Christ. We do not do justice to celibacy when we present it as being just the sacrifice of marriage for the sake of leaving oneself

---

[2] David M. KNIGHT, "Celibacy as a Personal Response," *The American Ecclesiastical Review*, Vol. CLXI, No. 6, (December, 1969), pp. 382-383.

more time — or even more freedom — to work for
the Kingdom of God. Such a celibacy suggests that of
the French Foreign Legion: the austere condition of
men who give up marriage and comfort to live an en-
forced bachelorhood in the desert, campaigning for
"la gloire de la France". The celibate does not give
up the personal values of married love just for the
sake of work, even work for the Kingdom of God.
Celibacy is itself a personal value, an intensification
of values on the level of personal relationship because
it is a unique relationship with the person of Christ.

Celibacy not contempt for the flesh

Nor is celibacy a "purer" way to live — as if it
were "more spiritual" or "more chaste" not to marry.
It is true that there were centuries of our tradition
during which Christian attitudes and values were
heavily flavored with pagan and neo-platonic contempt for the body. There are pages of Christian
writing that speak of sexual pleasure as being impure
by its very nature.[3] These writings may have been
existentially true; that is, they may have been quite
accurate commentaries on the concrete reality of the
sexual experience of the men for whose day they
were written. Men like St. Augustine came out of
a culture which did not understand or appreciate at
their proper value either women or sexual relationships. Theirs was a culture that had not yet evolved,
as ours has, through centuries of human dialogue with
Chrstian thought. I do not mean that our culture,
taken as a whole, is any more desirable by Christian
standards than theirs was. But our culture has grown
up with the leaven, the ferment of Christianity

[3] See Joseph E. KERNS, S.J., *The Theology of Marriage,*
New York (Sheed and Ward), 1964) chapter 4, for citations
and commentary.

working within it for a longer time. Our culture necessarily reveals an interacting with, expresses a response to, Christian values. The response can be negative or positive, authentic or distorted, but it is there. And so, even while we as a culture express contempt and lack of appreciation for the human body through genocide, torture of prisoners, abortion, sexual license, pornography, oppression of the poor, and crimes of violence, we nevertheless affirm passionately at the same time the value of personal self-expression, the equality of women, the nature of sexual relations as the expression of interpersonal love, and the dignity of human flesh. We have evolved in our thinking through many cultural movements, good and bad. We have been shaped through our acceptance of, and through our debates with, such historical movements as neo-platonism, manicheeism, the Renaissance, the Romantic Movement, Puritanism, feminism, and personalism, just to mention a random sampling. This means that in our day it is no longer possible for an informed Christian to reflectively think of sex simply as of an animal pleasure ordained to induce men to procreate. There was an age in which sex was experienced as something shameful by nature, and thought of as having no real value in itself — only the value of its consequences (procreation). Thus if one wasn't really needed for procreation, the only reason to marry would be for the sake of personal indulgence. In such a context sexual abstinence for the sake of God — no matter how it was understood — would appear to be, by its very nature, a "more perfect thing" than marriage for the sake of "sexual indulgence."

In this context the vow of celibacy would appear quite naturally as a vow to be more pure, more chaste, more spiritual than those people who involved their bodies in sexual pleasure. This is no longer the case.

We see sexual intercourse today as the expression of personal relationship between two people. Any defense of celibacy today must take as its starting point the definition of sex as sexual expression, not as sexual indulgence.

Celibacy not just freedom from distractions

Finally, celibacy cannot be sufficiently defended today on grounds that it leaves a person's mind and emotions more free for concentration on the things of the Lord. This argument was accepted almost as a self-evident presupposition in the past. To marry was to involve oneself in this world which is passing away. To be celibate was to free one's mind and heart for total absorption in the Lord. On these grounds St. Augustine argued that "only those who lack self-control should marry."[4] Marriage was necessary for some as a "remedy for concupiscence." (As St. Paul says, "If they cannot exercise self-control, they should marry. It is better to marry than to be on fire." (I Cor. 7: 9). But ideally the Christian should remain unmarried in order to concentrate exclusively on the Lord. In the eyes of these men it was marriage that required justification, not celibacy. To "be a eunuch for the Kingdom of God" was the normal thing for a Christian to do. And those who could accept it should accept it. (Cf. Mat. 19: 12).

Tertullian's argument for celibacy was that the Lord was coming soon. And who would want, at His coming, to be encumbered with the "baggage" of wife and children?[5] All of this is an echo, of course, of St. Paul's teaching that "the unmarried man is busy with the Lord's affairs, concerned with pleasing the

---

[4] KERNS, op. cit., chapter 7, note 12, p. 103.
[5] KERNS, op. cit., chapter 7, note 7, pp. 101-102. See the rest of the chapter for further amplification and citations.

Lord; but the married man is busy with this world's demands and occupied with pleasing his wife. This means he is divided." (I Cor. 7: 32).

We do not mean to contradict St. Paul, of course. But Paul's teaching, taken in its context, is less an explicit teaching about celibacy as such than it is a general teaching against being in any way divided in one's allegiance to the Lord, or distracted from the attention that should be given to His word. It is obviously better to be a celibate intent on the Lord than a married person intent on the things of this world. But it is also possible to be married person doubly intent on the Lord through the support one finds in one's spouse. Married couples can be a community of faith and prayer just as truly as religious can. In many instances they seem to be achieving this much better than religious.

It is ironic that in our day the reality of celibacy seems to be for so many the direct opposite of freedom to concentrate on the Lord. Celibates are freed from the concerns of marriage and children only to be swallowed up even more absorbingly by the demands of professional work. Instead of being free to "concentrate on prayer and the ministry of the word" (Acts 6: 4), priests and religious complain in chorus that they never have time to pray, to spend the Sabbath day in leisure, or even to make a retreat that isn't wedged in so tightly between high-pressure activities that real prayer is almost impossible. Where the married man of St. Paul's acquaintance was solicitous about his wife, the priest or religious of today is solicitous about committee meetings, job contracts, and social activism. Assess the value of these activities as you will; appeal to the impossibility of avoiding them; the fact remains that the celibate cannot defend his vocation today on grounds that it automatically leaves him more freedom to pray. One of the greatest problems in the Church is that so few celibates take time to pray at all.

Celibacy is positive, physical self-expression

The ancient tradition may seem to argue for celibacy on negative grounds, as removing the obstacles of family and flesh. But even at its most negative, the ancient tradition always presented celibacy as a way of living to the Lord, of relating personally to God in knowledge and mutual gift of self. And so celibacy is not, in its deepest and most authentic meaning, essentially a movement *away* from anything. Celibacy is not authentically understood as a movement away from sexual activity considered as a distraction from the Lord. Celibacy is not a movement away from personal love for the sake of more total dedication to work. Celibacy is not a movement away from man's affective or physical dimension, as if the body were an obstacle to the soul. Celibacy is not repression; it is expression. And the medium of celibate expression is the body.[6]

What we are undertaking to explain is that celibacy is an abiding physical response, enfleshed in the very abstinence of the body, to the person of Jesus Christ. Our physical stance of renunciation toward all potential partners in marriage on this earth both defines and expresses the nature of our response to Christ. It is a response to God offering Himself in Christ as partner in a relationship of love and friendship. This relationship is one of love and friendship on this earth, here and now. And it is human as well as divine.

[6] Celibacy as a self-creating act of personal expression is explained in my article "Celibacy as a Personal Response," *The American Ecclesiastical Review*, Vol. CLXI, No. 6. (December, 1969), pp. 375-385.

Celibacy expresses spousal relationship

What celibacy expresses is spousal relationship with Christ. It is a way of saying (and this is essentially its value), a way of saying in a physical, a real-symbolic way, that it is possible to have with Jesus Christ Himself, as person, a relationship of love and friendship in this life that is just as *real* as the relationship of spousal love in marriage. And it says that this relationship can be just as *satisfying* as the love-relationship of marriage. Furthermore, it says that this relationship is just as *developmental* of one's self as a loving person as spousal love can be in marriage.

Celibacy does not say that Christ *cannot* be found and loved in another, in other people, in a husband or wife. It says that He *can* be found and loved in Himself. It says that Jesus Himself is real. and available as the subject and object of a truly operative relationship of spousal love on this earth that does not have to pass through the intermediary of another who is husband or wife in order to be real.

All Christians believe this, of course, in theory. It is the very meaning of the Incarnation, of our doctrine of grace and divine indwelling. God became man in order to be knowable to us as Friend. Jesus is Emmanuel, God-with-us. But it is one thing to believe theoretically that in Christ God can be known and loved in real, growing, personal, human friendship. It is another thing to believe it in practice. To believe in practice is to invest something in our belief.

A Baptist minister once announced that he was going to push a wheelbarrow full of bricks across a tightrope stretched over Niagara Falls. A crowd gathered. Someone tried to dissuade him: "You can't do it; you'll be killed." But he did do it. And when he had crossed over and back, pushing his wheelbarrow, he questioned his skeptical friend: "Now do you believe I can do it?" "Yes," the man answered. "Do you really believe?" "Yes, I do."

"Then get in the wheelbarrow."

If all Christians just affirmed in words that it is possible to grow in knowledge and love of God in this life, but no one ever *staked* anything on that affirmation, the Christian belief would not be real. If everyone said it is possible to have the deepest relationship of human intimacy with Christ on this earth, but in fact no one were willing to be without the relationship of human love in marriage, what would this say about the reality of our faith?

The man who believes a party is going to be fun doesn't have to take a book along. If everyone gathered for a celebration and each person were found to have brought some reading material along "just in case", there would be an obvious lack of faith in the party. And so, if every Christian said, "Christ is my enough", but every Christian in fact provided himself with a wife or husband as well, it would be obvious that we don't believe Christ is enough to satisfy our need for human love in this life.

We are not suggesting here that married people only know Christ in and through other people while religious know Him in Himself, directly. Married people obviously can and do know Christ directly and in Himself. We can be excused, I hope, for not trying to explain married spirituality in a book on religious life. What we are saying here, and will explain, is that celibacy is a unique relationship with Christ. It expresses, establishes, and makes real a specific and unique relationship of spousal love with Jesus Christ on this earth. This will be our topic in this and the following chapter.

The expression "bride of Christ"

There is a fundamental problem, of course, about speaking of celibacy as spousal relationship with Christ. In what sense can we say that any group of Christians have a "spousal relationship with Christ" distinct from that of all Christians? There is only one Bride of Christ: the Church. And all the baptized, by the fact of their incorporation into the Church, become "brides in the Bride". The Fathers of the Church dwelt on the theme that there is only one Son of God: Jesus Christ, the only-begotten Son of the Father. But all who have been made members of Christ by Baptism are "sons in the Son, *filii in Filio*". It is in this sense that all are brides of Christ, brides in the Bride.

The expression "bride of Christ" is not popular today, because of the sentimentality that has been associated with it. But we cannot drop the expression without losing a thread that runs all through Scripture. And if we stop speaking of spousal relationship with Christ on the level of individuals we have to stop reading the mystics, because this is the imagery and language they use. St. John of the Cross, man that he was, expresses himself in the person of the bride when he addresses Christ. There is a sense in which all of us are "anima" before God.

Relationship based on baptism

The spousal relationship of every Christian with God through Christ is based on a specific commitment to a concrete way of acting. This is because every real relationship of love is based on interaction and commitment, as we will explain in the next chapter. In Baptism we commit ourselves to acting in a way that will lead us, eventually, to the Nuptials of the Lamb, to perfect union of mind and heart and will with God in the Beatific Vision in Heaven. And since spousal love is essentially a commitment to strive for perfect union of mind and will and heart, as we will explain below, the commitment of Baptism is essentially spousal.

Relationship embodied in a way of life

But a person might not really *embody* this spousal relationship in his life in any specific or recognizable way. Many of the baptized aim only at "saving their souls"; that is, at avoiding any sin so serious that it would keep them out of Heaven. In the measure that their theology is acceptable, and that one really can save his soul by aiming at nothing more than that, they can be said to be constituted in a real spousal relationship with Christ, to be really orienting their lives toward the Nuptials of the Lamb. But that doesn't make the spousal relationship appear. Nothing actually going on in their lives, here and now, would *express* a real decision to actually live to Christ on this earth in that specific way in which spouses commit themselves to live toward one another. Spousal love is a commitment to *work* at becoming one in mind and heart and will with another. It is a commitment to specific, concrete ways of doing this. But how many baptized Christians can say they are truly working — specifically and seriously — toward perfect union of mind and will and heart with God right now? The Christians we refer to as "born Catholics" are truly "brides in the Bride" because they have been baptized. But the reality of their spousal relationship with Christ is frequently like that of the children of royal families in the past who used to be married to each other while they were infants. Juridically, they were married. But they did not begin to interact with each other as man and wife until adulthood. They were juridically spouses, committed to start working, eventually, toward achieving union of mind and heart. But this commitment found no embodiment in their lives until they actually began to live together. Their spousal relationship was real only in a technical sense. So long as they were children, it could not be *realized*.

Then there are Christians who really have come to know the Lord, who are working toward perfect response to Him. Does this alone suffice to embody, to give specific form to, the spousal relationship of Baptism here in this life?

Spousal love is a concrete commitment

No. Spousal relationship is a very specific relationship, and requires some very specific commitments in order to stand out as real. It is not just a commitment to "perfect love." If it were, we would have a problem with spousal commitment between men and women in marriage, because all Christians are committed at Baptism to love *all* men perfectly. Hence no one can promise to love somebody *more* than anyone else, because we are all committed to loving everyone perfectly. When we enter into spousal relationship with a particular individual we do so by committing ourselves to specific ways of *acting* toward that individual on this earth. *These ways of acting are those which, in virtue of what they are in themselves, tend to bring people to perfect union of mind and will and heart.* Spousal relationship is real, not when we accept union with others as a *goal*, but when we *commit* ourselves to certain specific, concrete ways of acting as a *means* to accomplish this goal. And these means must be those which, of themselves, are directly and specifically ordered to the goal.

The actions which constitute the material of spousal commitment are those which of themselves lead to perfect, realized union of mind and heart and will. Keeping the commandments does not, of itself, lead to this kind of union with God on this earth or speak of spousal relationship with God. God might grant the Beatific Vision (which is perfect union with Himself) to those who have kept the commandments, but this would be a reward of God's choosing, not something which good moral conduct as such is inherently ordered to. But when two people on earth commit themselves to living together, to sharing their whole lives with each other, to communicating deeply day after day, to working at becoming totally unselfish toward one another, and to expressing this commitment in passionate, physical ways, this is a commitment to actions that of themselves lead to union of mind and will and heart. And these are the specific actions that celibates commit themselves to in regard to the person of Jesus Christ, as we will explain in our next chapter. These are not actions to which every Christian commits himself at Baptism; or if they are, it is only in an implicit way.

Spousal love is a one-to-one commitment

The question arises: Could not one enter into a spousal relationship with more than one person at a time? Could not a married person also have, and embody in his life on this earth, a spousal relationship with Christ as well as with his wife or husband?

The answer is no. Spousal relationship is by nature exclusive on this earth — not because it wants to be, but because it cannot be anything else. The reason for this is found in the limitations placed on human beings by the fact that we have bodies, and by the consequent fact that we must live and act in time and space. One cannot really talk deeply with two people at the same time. One cannot be simultaneously with two people who are in different places. One cannot commit oneself to yield simultaneously to the preferences of two different people who might ask for two contrary things. One cannot promise to follow two different people wherever they go unless it is certain they will be going in the same direction. And since people might go in different directions that are equally good, if one is committed to following two people, one of them is obviously going to have to have a personal priority over the other. It may be that in Heaven we can realize total spousal union with all other persons as well as with God. In the life to come there is no marrying or giving in marriage because all are like the angels in Heaven; that is, not subject to the limitations of time and space, able to be fully and equally present to everyone at the same time. But in this life we must specialize; we must commit ourselves to one person if we are going to be totally given in mind and will and heart to anyone.

Spousal love commits the body

This is why spousal commitment is so much a commitment of the *body,* and why it is properly and characteristically expressed by the gift of the body in sex. The spirit is willing to be given to all men at once, but the flesh limits us to one, if the gift is to mean anything. In marriage we commit our bodies to one person with priority — and that means giving him or her priority over every physical action which we are free to commit to another. We give *time,* for example, to communicating with our wife or husband first of all, and to all others in whatever measure is possible after that. We remain physically present in the first place to the one who is our spouse, living with that person in whatever place he might be, following him wherever he goes. When there is question of yielding to another's preference, we yield to the preference of our husband or wife before that of anyone else. This is what it means to accept another as a spouse. We recognize the limitations on our physical activity in this life and we commit ourselves physically to another. Spiritually our love should embrace the whole world. Our *concern* for others, and our desire to be *given* to others should be unlimited. But when it comes to actually living out, in the flesh, our love for other people, we are subject to the limitations of time and space. Marriage commits us to giving ourselves first of all to our spouse, and this in a total way. Everyone else has only a secondary claim on our bodily activity.

Giving Christ priority over the body

Since man from his side acts in space and time even when he is acting toward God, this limitation on man's physical activity carries over to our relationship with Christ. We cannot, at one and the same time, communicate deeply with Christ in prayer and with another human being in conversation. We cannot go somewhere and do something for Christ because we think He wants it, and at the same time yield to the preference of another human being that we go somewhere else and do some other thing. It follows then, that when it comes to *embodying,* to living out in physical actions, a spousal relationship during this life, one must choose between Christ and others, just as one would have to choose between any two human beings on earth. In the celibate commitment we give Christ priority over the time and space of our lives. And we seal this covenant by consecrating to him alone that power of symbolic expression in sex which is the characteristic expression of the commitment of one's body, and of one's physical activity, to another. The celibate is not committed specifically to communicating deeply all of his life with any individual person other than the person of God as revealed in Jesus Christ. No individual can claim priority over the when and where of a celibate's activity except Christ. The celibate may give up this or that moment of prayer to talk to another person in need, just as husbands and wives will give up moments of communication with each other to respond to another person's need. And other persons may claim moments of a celibate's time in the name of Jesus Christ. But when it comes to a choice, no one on earth can claim *personal priority* over the time and space of a celibate's being the way a spouse can claim this in marriage.

The priority of a spouse

Is this to say that in the lives of married people someone is given priority over Christ, over God? In a sense that is true, but let us not cry idolatry too soon. No Christian gives anyone priority over God when there is question of a choice between obeying God or man. But there is a *kind* of priority over God's will in our lives that we can give to others by God's own arrangement. In marriage a man leaves father and mother and clings to his wife. His parents must release their claims on him, in the sense that his wife now has first claim, not on his love, but on his body and its physical activity in time and space. God also releases His claims over us, in a similar way, when we marry. If God were to call a person to some special service, for example, that the person's spouse absolutely refused to accept, God's own law of marriage could require that person to give priority to his spouse. We are assuming here, of course, that no question of sin or of obligations that bind under sin is involved. No husband or wife could forbid the other to pray; but either spouse could claim priority over the other's time at any given moment and insist on conversation rather than prayer. A wife might discern a call from God Himself to live in a poor neighborhood as an expression of Christian faith in the Beatitudes; her husband could veto that. A man might want to join a prayer group but have to forego it because it would cause division between himself and his wife. A celibate religious in these situations would be subject to no one except Jesus Christ. It is true that the celibate must often forego some direct response to Christ out of charity toward others, or in obedience to superiors. But no one can claim this of him on grounds of personal priority, as a spouse is able to do. A religious is not even in a relationship of person-to-person commitment to his superior. Spouses commit themselves to each other by name — to make clear that the commitment is to this unique, individual person as such. "I, John, take you, Mary." But religious commit themselves to their superior by *title,* to make clear that the bond is not between these two unique human beings as such, but between the religious and the person of Jesus Christ, as represented by whatever human being happens to hold the office of superior at a given time. The bond of commitment on this earth ceases to exist between married persons when one of them dies. The bond of a religious is unaffected by the death of his superior, because it is not between the religious and the person of the superior as such. Thus there is no concrete person to whom a religious is directly and permanently committed in this life the way spouses are to one another. The religious makes the commitment of his body, and of all its activity, to Jesus Christ Himself as Spouse.

Indirect commitment to fellow religious

Here we have one of the clearest distinctions between the commitment one makes to a spouse in marriage and the commitment one has toward the other members in a religious community. In marriage one's commitment is directly to the person of one's spouse, "for better or worse." In religious life one has no direct commitment even to the members of one's order, but only the indirect commitment that follows as the natural result of committing oneself to Christ as a member of this particular community. The religious takes his vows to Christ, to live according to the Constitutions and Institute of a given religious congregation. This involves him in community with all others who have made or will make the same commitment. Since the members of the community mutually condition each others' lives and responses to Christ, the commitment of each one to live by the Rule involves a responsibility and commitment toward every other member and toward the community as a whole. But this commitment is secondary. It is a consequence of each one's primary commitment to live to Christ according to the specific Rule of the Institute. There is no immediate primary commitment to the other members by name, as particular individuals. Should some member refuse to live by the Rule, he can be expelled. No one is committed directly to living with him as an individual person, but only indirectly, through the common commitment all have to live the community's way of life together. And should the community as a whole fail to live by the Rule, no one is committed to remain in it. A religious must ask permission of the Church to transfer to another community, and he must remain faithful to his religious vows (since they were made to Christ, and not to the community), but he has no direct commitment to remain with this particular group of people. In fact, God might call him to leave a very fervent community in order to join or to found another. His commitment is to Christ, and not to the members of his order. In this religious life is very different from marriage, in which two individual persons are committed directly to each other as such, and neither can expel or leave the other without breaking off the marital relationship and rendering the spousal commitment itself inoperative.

It has been the purpose of this chapter to show that the vow of celibacy in religious life is a real-symbolic, embodied expression of a commitment to living out in human operations a spousal relationship with Christ. It is a commitment to giving visible embodiment on this earth, in concrete, specific actions, to the essentially spousal commitment that all Christians have with God through Baptism. As such it is an expression, in real-symbolic gesture, of the reality of grace that is within us.

The relationship of the celibate to the rest of the Church

Because celibacy embodies something that is a basic reality in every Christian's life, the vocation to celibacy is not some private, personal gift that is both irrelevant and unrelated to the lives of other Christians. It is rather a way of life that is of service to the whole Church, just by being what it is. For celibacy as a way of life reveals to every Christian something of what he is, something of his own relationship with God. No Christian lifestyle can embody the whole reality of grace. Every Christian way of life reveals an aspect — and only an aspect — of the mystery of Christian life as such, and in so doing reveals to every other Christian something of what he is. The celibate's vocation in the Church is to call attention to the Nuptials that are to come, by embodying already in this life a specific, spousal relationship to Christ in concrete ways. In doing this the celibate also expresses, radically and unambiguously, the Christian belief that in Jesus Christ God has drawn near to us as Person — so near that He can be for us, even on earth, the object of a real, an authentic relationship of spousal love already actualized during this life.[7]

It remains for us now to explain more in detail what the spousal commitment to Christ actually entails.

[7] What celibacy "says" to non-celibate Christians about their own lives is further developed in my article "Will the New Church Need Celibates?", *New Catholic World*, Vol. 216, No. 1292, (Sept./Oct., 1973), pp. 207-211.

CHAPTER SIX

The Commitment of Spousal Love to Christ

Spousal love is first of all a *relationship*. Then it is a particular *kind* of relationship. So, in order to explain spousal relationship with Christ, we must first of all explain what makes relationships between persons real in the first place. Then we must explain what makes spousal relationship exist[1].

First of all, for any love relationship between persons to be real, it must be founded on *interaction*. I might say in my heart that I "love all men". But I don't have a real relationship of love with any man until I *do* something that expresses love for that man. In doing something loving for someone I "realize" my love for him: I discover it and make it real.

If we are speaking of a *stable* relationship between persons, then it must be founded on *commitment*. I am constituted in an abiding relationship of love toward another person when I am committed to act toward that person — and to keep acting toward him — in a certain way. A passing act of kindness to a stranger in need might express an habitual attitude of love (and commitment) toward my fellowman in general. But when we speak of specific, real relation-

---

[1] This topic is also developed in my article "Spousal Commitment in Religious Life," *Review for Religious*, Vol. 32, No. 1, (January, 1973), pp. 85-96.

ships of love between persons, we are speaking not of passing acts but of commitments.

The *kind* of commitment one makes to another determines the kind of love-relationship one enters into with him. A parent commits himself to provide for his children, to educate and defend them, and to invest his whole being in their development. But a parent does not commit himself to sharing his whole mind and heart with his children in the way he does with his spouse. A feudal serf engaged himself to love his lord, to obey his commands and die in his service if necessary. But he did not aspire to intimacy with his lord.

Definition of spousal love

To what do a husband and wife commit themselves in spousal love? I think it should be clear in our age that spousal love is a commitment to doing toward another, for one's whole life, all of those things that tend, of themselves, to bring two people to *perfect union* of mind, and will, and heart.

I believe we can say that such a commitment involves at least four things: *living together, communication, conversion* to each other's ideals, and the *physical expression* of love. In a loose and overlapping way we can match the first two with the goal of union of minds, the third with union of wills, and the fourth with union of hearts.

Continuous presence to each other

Living together is essential to spousal love because real union of mind and heart between two persons is arrived at through sharing and reflecting together on all the experiences of life as they shape and challenge the being of each one. This is one of the reasons why spousal love is limited to a one-to-one relationship on this earth; because people cannot live in more than one place at a time so long as they are subject to the conditions of time and space that pertain to physical existence. If two people are not able to promise that consistent physical presence to one another that is required for continuous interaction on this earth, there is no way that they will be able to bring together, integrate, and harmonize with each other all those experiences and responses to life that change and develop the personality of each over the course of the years. Unless they keep interacting with one another as each one changes, they will grow apart instead of growing together.

In religious life there is no one person we are really pledged to *being with* in this way other than the person of Christ (involving, of course, all Three Persons of the Trinity, Father, Son, and Spirit). In active orders members are constantly being transferred from house to house. Even in monasteries with a vow of stability, not only is it quite possible that someone might be asked to go with a group beginning a new foundation, but even within the monastery there is no individual member of the community with whom one is committed to bringing together and sharing all of the experiences of the day throughout one's whole life. But in religious life there is such a commitment to bring each day with its experiences into the presence of Christ. It is usually a very concrete commitment, expressed in some very specific, identifiable, and even structured engagements. There is a kind of prayer that belongs to religious life — it takes different forms and has different names: it is called recollection, review of life, examination of conscience, consciousness examen[2], discernment of spirits, in-

---

[2] See George ASCHENBRENNER, S.J., "Consciousness Examen", *Review for Religious*, vol. 31, (1972), No. 1, pp. 14-21.

teriorization, the pursuit of self-knowledge (or the refusal to escape the self-knowledge that pursues of itself the man who goes into the solitude of prayer). It can be called by many names, but its reality is the same: it is prayer that consists in bringing into the presence of Christ all the experiences, insights, and responses of our day, year after year, letting His responses mesh or clash with our own, until finally we are rubbed and polished into perfect conformity with His mind and will and heart. This can be abrasive, of course. Sometimes it can be more than abrasive; it can depth-charge the secret recesses of our souls, the subterranean caves where our true selves lurk away in hiding from the monsters that terrorize the deep. In the company of Christ we confront each monster as it comes, even Grendel in her cave, until the peace of Christ is established down to the very center of our earth. This is what it means to "live together" with Christ, interacting with Him over all the events of our lives, day after day.

Union of mind

Communication is the circulatory system that gives life to any spousal relationship. Two people who do not *talk deeply* to one another can have no commitment to arrive at union of mind and heart. Where marriage is not understood as a mutual engagement to keep communicating, to keep trying to break through the barriers that keep us from understanding one another, the true nature of marriage as spousal love is not understood. The man who does not talk deeply to his wife has not really accepted her as a person; he is not interested in achieving union with her on the level of her personhood. That is why married couples who stop trying to communicate with one another in depth are violating their marriage vows. The standard textbooks teach that it is serious sin for a wife to deny her body to her husband without cause. To deny one's mind to one's spouse is even more serious, because the surrender of the body in intercourse, as we will see below, is only a symbolic expression of the interior commitment to open the deepest recesses of one's mind and heart to another forever.

Celibacy without commitment to a lifelong communication with Christ in prayer would be unintelligible, inconceivable as a Christian engagement. The very meaning of celibacy would be denied at its root. For celibacy says that it is possible to grow in knowledge and love of Christ on earth just as really as one can grow in knowledge and love of a spouse in marriage. But without communication there is no growth in knowledge and love between persons. And prayer is the main artery of our communication with Christ, with God.

The Church has never, to my limited historical knowledge, given her approval to the vow of celibacy as a way of life for any Christian who did not at the same time engage himself to a life of prayer. In our own day it is hardly thinkable that anyone could envisage religious life without this including a constant praying over the Scriptures. The word of God is given first place in Vatican II's insistence on the life of prayer proper to religious.[3] And so the time formally committed to meditation and prayer in a religious community is a specific, concrete expression of the

---

[3] "Decree on the Appropriate Renewal of the Religious Life", par. 6: "Therefore, drawing on the authentic sources of Christian spirituality, let the members of communities energetically cultivate the spirit of prayer and the practice of it. In the first place they should take the sacred Scriptures in hand each day by way of attaining 'the excelling knowledge of Jesus Christ' (Phil. 3: 8) through reading these divine writings and meditating on them." (Abbott, pg. 471).

commitment each member has to communicate with
the person of Jesus Christ his whole life long in search
of union of mind and will and heart with Him.

Union of will

A *conversion of attitudes and values* to embrace
whatever is best and most beautiful in the vision and
ideals of one's spouse is essential, of course, if married
couples are going to arrive at perfect union of will
with each other. Union of will means commitment to
the same goals, the same ideals. It involves a commitment to give in to another's preferences at times,
for the sake of unity. But where division occurs
on the level of ideals, no Christian can commit
himself to giving up the higher for the lower.
We cannot promise to do what is evil. And to
bind oneself to accept another's attitudes and
values, even when they are less idealistic than
one's own, would be to make that other person
one's god. So spousal love between humans means that
each is pledged to accept whatever is best and more
beautiful in the vision and idealism of the other, so
that both come together in unity by rising upwards
in response to each other.

In the spousal relationship with Christ, it is His
ideals and values which are, by definition, better. He
is our God. And so we pledge ourselves to a continual
conversion of our own attitudes and values to bring
them into conformity with His own in the measure
that we come to understand Him.

This is not just a vague, general sort of commitment to "do good and avoid evil". It is a specific
engagement with a concrete person, and to a particular relationship with that person. Our spousal
commitment to Christ binds us to *express* in concrete
ways, real ways, the sincerity of our purpose to come

to union of wills with Him. All of the forms of prayer we mentioned above express this purpose: mental prayer, examination of consciousness or of conscience, the effort to interiorize and integrate with Christ all of the experiences and growth of each day. The use of confession expresses this purpose, as does the use of spiritual direction and of spiritual government. Retreats and days of solitude express it. Spiritual reading and study of the Scriptures express it, when such reading or study is undertaken precisely with the purpose of letting the words one reads, and especially the Word of God, call one's life into question. In fact we can say that, for a Christian, to study the Scriptures over a long period of time with any other goal than that of letting them call one's own life into question is to incur the risk of losing the faith. The Scriptures are not just a book to be studied; they are a voice to respond to. To study them without adverting to that voice is to implicitly deny the living God who speaks through His Word. (That is why we sometimes see theologians losing the faith).

Do the religious vows commit us any more than Baptism does to a total conversion of our wills to God's? I suppose that to answer this in real theological depth would require us to take a position on just what the commitment of Baptism actually entails. But on the level of ordinary understanding, and especially on the level of the psychological, personal reality of our commitment, I think the answer is obvious. Theoretically, Christians are already pledged — by Baptism itself — to work toward perfect unity of wills with each other and with Christ. We are to be one as Christ and the Father are one. But the general commitment of Baptism doesn't seem to be enough. And so we spontaneously re-commit ourselves in specific ways. When two people marry, for example, they are conscious of engaging themselves in relationship to each other to work for this unity in a special way, or with a particular intensity and perseverance of effort. This is what marriage is: a direct and persevering effort to achieve unity with one other person, conscious that this very unity, if attained through the raising and not the lowering of our ideals, will bring us into closer unity with all others who are likewise rising upwards in response to one another. All that rises leads to Christ, where all goodness and truth is united, and where all will be one in One. And so the religious vows, like the marriage vows, specify the general baptismal commitment to love by adding to it a specific engagement to strive through concrete efforts to arrive at perfect unity of mind and heart and will with one particular person, and through that unity to grow toward unity with all. Through the marriage vows we form this relationship visibly with another human being on earth. Through the vow of celibacy we enter into that same relationship just as visibly with the invisible person of Christ.

What makes this relationship particularly *visible* is celibacy: By the visible stance of renunciation taken toward all other possible objects of spousal love on earth we proclaim and manifest the reality and availability of Jesus Christ precisely as object of such a relationship. And at the same time we manifest the reality of our turning toward Christ as the one with whom we have determined to enter into this relationship.

Aren't we committed by Baptism itself to a total conformity of will to God? I suppose we are. But this does not mean that on the psychological level of one's personal realization and conscious determination every baptized Christian understands himself as being actually engaged in arriving at perfect surrender of his will to God's. Many — perhaps most — baptized Christians would say, if questioned, that all they really feel they have personally accepted as their religious commitment is to avoid serious sin, stay out of Hell, and get into Heaven.

But when these Christians marry, they begin to understand what love is all about, because they must work at giving themselves totally to their spouses. Any person whose highest ideal in marriage were just "not to get divorced", or not to be unfaithful to his spouse by adultery, would hardly be living up to his marriage vows. And so marriage teaches us something about our baptismal commitment to God by giving us the experience of what it is to be *concretely* committed to another, visible, particular, individual human being on earth. For religious, the vow of celibacy is a way of adding to our baptism precisely that note of conscious, explicit, concrete commitment to Jesus Christ as object of spousal relationship on this earth. It is a specific engagement, taken as adults, to go all the way with Him in love, the way spouses commit themselves to respond totally and without reserves to one another.

Union of heart

The physical expression of love in sexual relations is integral to the relationship of spouses in marriage. People are not "one heart and soul" with each other just through cold, rational commitment to the same goals in life. Union of wills becomes union of heart when some passion, some mutual, heartfelt emotion is experienced between persons. Likewise, human beings do not *know* other persons, or express themselves to others, just through the airways of intellectual discussion. People *act* to show love, and they touch. The deep, emotional touching of sexual relations is an integral part of marriage. It expresses the "heart", which is a meeting-ground of mind, emotions and will. Thus it expresses in a unique way the kind of love spouses have pledged to each other.

A deeper understanding of sex than is current in our society is essential if we are to understand either marriage or celibacy. The day is long gone, I hope, when sex was taught as something fundamentally degrading to the spirit of man. And yet some of the Fathers of the Church were so conscious of the bodily pleasure and loss of rational control inherent in the sex act that they taught it was an action always shameful: even sinful in itself because of the absorption in pleasure it involved. It was saved from sinfulness in marriage only if sexual relations were sought for the sole motive of producing children.[4]

The "trap and bait" theory

In my own lifetime — and for all I know it still goes on today — the value of sex, and the moral principles governing its use, were taught according to the "trap and bait" theory. According to this theory the end of sex is children: this is what God really wants. But the proper rearing of children requires marriage. And so, to induce people to enter into marriage and raise children, God gives human beings a very strong physical appetite for sex. Sex is the bait. Marriage is the trap. Inside the trap you can have all the bait you want, provided you do not frustrate the purpose of the sexual act, which is children. Outside of the trap it is serious sin to steal the bait.[5]

---

[4] See KERNS, *op. cit.,* chapter 4, citing Justin the Martyr, St. Clement of Alexandria, St. Jerome, and St. Augustine.

[5] See KERNS, *op. cit.,* chapter 5, note 67, p. 78; Edwin F. Healy, S.J., *Moral Guidance* (Chicago, Loyola University Press, 1957), pp. 188-189; Gerald KELLY, S.J., *Modern Youth and Chastity* (Liguorian — Queen's Work pamphlets, 1964), esp. pp. 70-72.

The trap-and-bait explanation adds little to the anti-sexual attitude of the early Fathers. All it really does is stop condemning the bodily enjoyment of sexual pleasure as something shameful in itself. But physical pleasure, even when it is not considered shameful, is still not a value.[6] There is a constant tendency among human beings, especially when they begin to philosophize, to recognize more human value in asserting self-control over the desire for pleasure, or in sacrificing pleasure for a higher ideal, than in indulging in pleasure as such. In fact, human beings are a little leery of pleasure, especially of any pleasure with as much power as sex, which has the potential to take over man's will and rule his life. If the Fathers of the Church sound negative toward sex, it is my hypothesis that they were dealing with the reality of sex in their day, and that their Christianity made them much more positive in their attitudes toward sex than the pagan thinkers of their culture.

Sex is a language

But today society has evolved in its understanding of sex. Christianity may even have been responsible for the evolution. We no longer see sex as "pleasure and procreation, period!", any more than we see the role of woman in marriage as being just to serve the domestic and physical needs of her husband, drawing support from her piety in church for this essentially sacrificial role: the *"Kinder, Küche, und Kirche"* definition of the ideal wife. Men and women are equals in marriage, and their relationship is one of mutual sharing of mind and will and heart. In this relationship sex becomes a language. It is a language

---

[6] St. FRANCIS DE SALES, *Introduction to the Devout Life* (Image Books, 1955) Part III, ch. 39, # 4, p. 221. Kerns cites St. Thomas Aquinas on this, *op. cit.*, p. 58.

of physical, symbolic gestures. And what it expresses
is commitment. But to be this sex requires a context
of marriage understood as a relationship of spousal
love — an engagement to work toward total union
on the level of persons.

I was a missionary in Africa for three years,
working with a tribe that did not believe in the
equality of men and women. Even husbands and
wives did not eat together or try to communicate with
each other. As one man put it in a discussion group
on marriage: "Why should I ask my wife's opinion
about anything? I paid more for my oxen than I
paid for my wife, and I never ask my oxen's opinion
about anything!" Another man said, "I never ask my
wife's opinion about anything because in my opinion
my wife doesn't know anything!" (I discovered upon
my return to this country that the men of our own
western civilization are not always very different from
the African in their fundamental attitude toward their
wives). Obviously, in a relationship that does not involve a commitment to share one's mind and heart
with the other, sex can be little more than pleasure
and procreation. Where there is tenderness and
respect, the pleasure can be psychological as well as
physical, but the real, the intrinsic value of the sexual
act as such will still not be there.

What is this value? It is the value of *self-
expression*. Sex is the expression of one's freely
chosen stance toward another. It expresses self-gift.
It is not just the expression of emotion. Sometimes
we slip into thinking that sex just expresses something
we feel, a level of affectivity or intimacy already
achieved with another, or about to be achieved
through the sexual act itself. There is truth in this, of
course, but if this were the whole truth sex would
have no value as the expression of one's self. The
self is free. When we speak of man's self, his person,

we mean above all his freedom-in-action. Man's feelings are not truly his self until they are freely accepted and affirmed, until they become matters of free choice. Man's self is his constantly-evolving self-orientation, it is the self he is creating by his choices, the self he chooses to be. It is this self that finds expression above all in authentic sexual relations, because it is this self, and this self alone, who is the seat and source of love. And sex is the expression of love.

The expression of committed love

Love is a free act. It is something we promise in marriage "till death do us part". It is something we can even be commanded to give, as God commands us to love one another. If love were just a complex of feelings it could not be commanded or promised. Feelings are a "happening". They are a product of man as mechanisms. They cannot be willed into existence by man except indirectly, by his choice to do some things that might produce certain feelings. But love is a free stance of the will; it can be taken by choice, persevered in by fidelity. Therefore it can be commanded and promised. It is normal and desirable that emotions accompany love, but these cannot be counted on, at least not constantly. St. Teresa of Avila, passionate mystic that she was, points out repeatedly: "Love consists, not in the extent of our feelings of contentment *(gusto)*, but in the *firmness of our determination*".[7]

Love is commitment. And every love-relationship is a particular stance of commitment toward another. The intrinsic value of the sexual act as such, apart from the results that follow from it (its extrinsic value,

[7] *Interior Castle*, Fourth Mansions, chapter 1, par. 7, (in E. A. PEERS, Image Books, 1961, p. 76).

procreation), is just that sexual relations are a passionate expression of commitment. And through the expression of commitment we grow in commitment. Sex is the real-symbolic expression of the committed gift of oneself in love. It helps us to "realize" — to discover and make real — deeper levels of self-giving. Sex normally involves, or should bring to consciousness, deep emotions. But essentially it is the expression, not of emotions, but of the will. Sexual intercourse is an embodied pledge. It is the gift of self enacted in dramatic, physical gestures. These gestures are "real-symbols", not in the sense that they cannot be rendered meaningless by falsity, but in the sense that they engage one's being more than words. No one passes through sexual intercourse unchanged. To deliver oneself to another in this way is to engage something real in one's act of self-expression; it is to put one's flesh and blood on the line in ways and with risks that no one can ever see fully or clearly in advance.

Such a risk is justified only in the name of life itself, which for human beings consists essentially in freedom. The supreme value of human existence is self-determination. And the highest act of self-determination is to commit oneself to another in love. For the sake of the exercise of this power of self-commitment any risk to oneself is justified except the risk of infidelity to commitments already made. (This includes one's commitment to God, of course). And so sexual gift of oneself to another as an act of free self-determination, as an expression of committed love, is worth the hazards of the unknown. It is an act of faith in the value and power of man's freedom to give himself into the future.[8]

[8] See John C. HAUGHEY, S.J., *Should Anyone Say Forever*, pp. 26-36.

The hypocrisy of shallow gestures

This is why sexual relations outside of marriage, outside of the context of committed, spousal love, are always wrong. They cannot be authentic; they are the enactment of a lie. If sexual relations are not the expression of commitment, they are not the expression of a person. If they do not express a free stance taken with the will, they can only be the expression of feeling toward another (or of something less than this, which we do not even consider here, such as bare physical or psychological self-gratification). But to reduce sexual expression to the expression of feeling alone is to strip sex of its intrinsic value. It is to make the authenticity of sex, even within marriage, depend on something beyond the control of persons. This might possibly explain why sometimes married couples feel dissatisfied with themselves after sex. If a woman, for example, is not feeling romantic but gives herself dutifully, or even generously, to her husband at his request — perhaps even faking enjoyment for the sake of her husband's feelings — she is liable to feel hypocritical, or even that she has been "used". If a man senses his wife's lack of feeling, he is liable to feel that he is in fact using her selfishly, with an accompanying reaction of contempt toward himself and resentment toward her. Then sex leaves an aftertaste of disgust.

It is to our purpose to point out here that this same misunderstanding of sex as being the expression of feeling rather than of commitment can also be found, with similar results, in the area of religious expression. The person whose underlying assumption, conscious or unconscious, is that prayer, or participation at Mass, or any other expression of devotion, is really an expression of *feeling* toward God or toward what is going on in a religious ceremony, is liable to experience discouragement through such

exercises — disgust toward himself, resentment toward
God because he "can't be what he is supposed to be"
when expressing himself to God. He feels that
"something is wrong" which it is beyond his power
to do anything about, and that therefore he "doesn't
belong" at prayer, or in church, and that it might
even be an act of hypocrisy for him to be there. At
the same time he feels resentment toward God because
he knows he *wants* to do the right thing, but whatever
that "right thing" is that people are supposed to find
in prayer, etc., it just does not seem to be available to
him.

Whether we are speaking of sexual expression or
of religious expression, the same misunderstanding
spins us off into despair. We have somehow fallen
into the error of thinking that sex and religion are
matters of feeling — perhaps because in both areas
those who are presented to us as having done them
well always seem to have found so much feeling in the
process. It is a shame that so many stories of sexual
love end at the wedding ceremony — when authentic
sexual love is just able to begin. And it is equally a
shame that so many stories about the Saints stress
their mystical experiences instead of their dark nights
of soul. Be that as it may, we must return to an authentic understanding of both sexual and religious acts
as being the expression of commitment. We express
through our bodies the free determination of our wills;
our response of engagement in self-orienting love
toward another person. An expression of commitment
can never be hypocritical so long as the commitment
is sincere. If my *determination* to be for another
what I presume to be is *real,* then the expression of
that determination, of that commitment, cannot be
hypocritical — no matter what feelings do or do not
accompany it. For two people who are really determined to live their marital commitment, intercourse
can never be hypocritical. For two people who are not

determined to live an existing marital commitment, intercourse is always hypocritical.

The symbolic language of sex

In sexual expression every physical gesture is a symbol. This is obvious and not obvious; taken for granted, yet not really understood. We are used to hearing that sex is the "expression of love" — so used to it that we do not challenge the connection. But what connection do the physical gestures of sex have with expressing love? Why should these gestures express only spousal love, and not just any level of affection toward another?

It is here that we have to think about sex as a language. As Frank Sheed once pointed out, people do not really think about sex. We talk about it, dream about it, phantasize about it, but we do not think about it. To think about sex means to ask what is behind the desires that we have, the gestures we are moved to engage in. What are we really looking for through and beyond the physical actions and pleasures of sex as such?

Nakedness of body — nakedness of soul

In Africa I was pastor of what might be called a "topless parish". Nudity was a normal thing. When I went there I expected this to be disturbing. But to my surprise it wasn't. And so, for the first time in my life I began to ask myself, "What is behind nudity in marriage? What is so sexual about it?"

Nudity in marriage is a symbolic gesture. It is a way of saying, "I pledge myself to be naked in mind and heart to you." We cannot totally reveal our minds, or the depths of our hearts, to another in one act.

Even if we could express everything we are conscious of within ourselves, we know that as the years go on we discover deeper and deeper levels of our souls — and that the depths are constantly growing deeper. But we can reveal our bodies, totally, all in one act. To do this as a pledge of continuing revelation of heart and mind is to be naked before another in sex. To be naked without this pledge is to say nothing that engages one's self. To be naked without such a pledge in a sexual context, is just to make oneself the object of another's pornographic interest. But to be naked freely and deliberately before another, as a pledge of one's determination to make oneself naked before that person in heart and soul forever, this is to express in language as beautiful as it is sexual the total gift of oneself to another in spousal love.

What is sexually exciting in the nakedness of marriage, then, is the fact and realization that, through this gesture, another *person* is expressing his or her willingness to share himself or herself totally with me in love.

Gift of the body — gift of self

What is true in marriage of nakedness is true of all of the physical gestures of marital sex. One gives one's body to the other as a way of saying that with this person there will be no reserves, there is no place to draw the line. In intercourse the body is surrendered completely as a sign of the total surrender of the person. And the man who takes his wife's body to himself in intercourse is expressing, not just a taking, but a giving, because the only reason he is able to take his wife to himself in marriage is that he has already taken her *unto* himself: to protect, shelter, provide for, and share his whole strength and being with her forever. His taking of her to himself physically is, in this context, the expression of the fact of his commitment.

Strip sexual gestures of the expression of commitment and you strip them of all intrinsic value. And truly sexual gestures — the gestures proper to sex as such — lose their objective symbolic meaning if they are not the expression of total gift — that is, of spousal love, the commitment to share oneself completely with another in a life that aims at total union of mind and heart and will. The language of sex is not the expression of a loan, or of partial gift, or of a level of intimacy already attained. It is a way of saying in passionate, symbolic gestures that one is pledging the total surrender and commitment of oneself to another.

Celibacy as physical expression of love

How can such a language, of passionate, physical expression, be found in the celibate life, in a relationship of spousal love with Christ?

All truly sexual expression is excluded, of course, from the celibate life. But if we look at the underlying reality of sexual expression, which is to be *physical, symbolic expression of total gift* of oneself to another, this reality can take other forms than those which we identify as sex. The crucifixion of Christ, for example, was a physical expression — and a passionate physical expression — of total gift of self to His Bride, the Church. The passionate physical penances of the Saints (where they were authentic and psychologically healthy) can hardly be understood except as passionate gestures of desire to be overcome by the grace of God and surrendered totally in love to Christ.

First of all we should admit that the very fact of celibacy itself, the continuing physical act of remaining continent and chaste, is a physical, symbolic gesture of total gift to Christ. A celibate is not a person who just happens not to have married yet. A celibate is someone who has made a definite, conscious act of consecrating all his sexual powers to continence precisely as an expression of spousal commitment to Christ. His free choice has taken the form of an abiding physical reality, which is continence or virginity. His physical state of continence is not just a fact: it is an enduring *act,* a word of free choice that has taken flesh in an abiding, irreversible gesture that is not only symbolic but real-symbolic in the clearest sense of the word.

Celibacy is a *passionate* physical expression to God. It takes passion to renounce passion, at least if the passion one renounces is felt, actual, and real. The celibate person can be sure that he will feel during much of his life the insistent passion of sexual desire. Persevering resistance to sexual temptation will require a passion of its own, and constitute in itself a quiet but authentically passionate experience of the measure of one's love for Christ.

Penance in the celibate life

We should not pass over the reality of physical penances as an expression of passionate love for Christ. The vocation to virginity has always been associated in Christian literature ·vith a call to prayer and penance.[9] It is true that what "penance" fundamentally means is interior penance, metanoia, a conversion of mind and heart to God. But the desire for this interior conversion finds expression in exterior

---

[9] Cf. for example, *Roman Missal,* Mass for the Blessing and Consecration of Virgins.

penance or penances, such as fasting, sleeping on boards, or causing pain to the body.[10]

Penance can be understood in many ways.[11] As *self-conquest,* physical penances are just stoic exercises through which reason gains dominance over anarchic passions. In itself this is not necessarily a religious act, although it can serve religious purposes. As *reparation* for sin — one's own or another's — penance could be understood as an almost pagan placation of the gods, as if the God revealed in Jesus Christ exacted payment, measured out in pain, as the price of one's forgiveness. This notion would seem to contradict our Lord's portrayal of the mercy of God in the parable of the Prodigal Son, in His own acts of forgiveness of Mary Magdalene, the Good Thief, etc. This kind of penance could, in our lives, spring psychologically from a sense of guilt and unpaid debt toward God. Or penance could be understood as a way of *asking a favor* from God — as if prayer addressed to God in faith were not enough, and God's favors must be "bought" through sacrifice and pain. These three ways of understanding penance are classical enough, but I believe they are a distortion of the real understanding the Saints had of penance in their lives.

Penance as symbolic gesture

Let us, then, call penance nothing but a *symbolic gesture* through which man allows the word of graced

---

[10] See St. IGNATIUS LOYOLA, *Spiritual Exercises,* Tenth Addition, paragraphs 82-86, in L. J. Puhl's translation (Loyola University Press, Chicago 1951), pp. 37-38.

[11] *Ibid.,* parag. 87, p. 38. Here we will take St. Ignatius's three reasons for doing penance, criticize them on one level of understanding, then reinterpret them on another level. Understood as three expressions of the heart through *symbolic gesture,* St. Ignatius's reasons for doing penance are perfectly valid today.

response in his heart to take flesh in actions capable
of expressing the gift of grace he has been given. If
this grace is a desire to be totally overcome by grace
and surrendered to God, he may do penance, and
even speak of it, in a way that suggests stoic self-
conquest. But he will really be expressing, not a
voluntaristic assertion of mind over matter, of intellect and will over emotion, but simply a *desire to
be overcome* — in his helplessness to overcome himself — by the all-subduing power of grace.

If the grace being expressed is sorrow for sins —
his own or those of others — he may do and speak
of penance as if he were "making up" to God for the
sins of the world. But in reality he will only be expressing his sorrow for sin, and for the hurt it has
caused to God, in a language more passionate than
words. God exacts no "payment" for sin. But man
exacts of himself an expression of his deepest heart
that is real, that is more than words and airy thoughts.
Man cannot refrain from letting the word of his love
take flesh. The man who has sinned in ways that
passionately involved his whole being — body,
emotions, and choices — is not satisfied that his
change of mind and direction can be really, can be
adequately expressed by a few words in confession
and a string of Hail Mary's. He wants to express his
return to God as convincingly as he expressed his rejection of God. This is what penance is.

Finally, if a man's grace is one of petition, he may
do penance as a way of asking something more in-
sistently of God. But the penance is not a bribe. In
the prayers we address to God it is faith and faith
alone that prevails. But our faith becomes operative
in the measure that we consciously draw upon the
power to believe that is within us. Penance is a way
of letting our faith become aware. When we join

fasting to prayer we realize how much we do care about the person or favor for which we are praying. We are "investing" something in our act of petition, something of flesh and blood, something that is real in addition to the words. This is a way of expressing confidence in the power of prayer, confidence that we really are speaking to someone who is there, who cares about us, who will hear us. We are not tossing off a few low-cost prayers "just in case", like someone sending out a few hundred mimeographed begging letters on the possibility that some might get a response. When we join penance to prayer we are spinning our petition out of our very insides, spinning our guts into a web to block God's path and call His attention to the earnestness of our request.

The excesses of the Saints

When penance is understood as self-expression, as the word of grace that is within us becoming flesh and blood in its expression, the *excesses* of the Saints begin to make sense. Constantly we hear that the Saints in their extreme penitential practices are "to be admired but not imitated". But this poses a problem. If what the Saints did was the direct inspiration of grace, how could it be that God would move them to something immoderate, something against reason (as they themselves admitted their penances often were)? On the other hand, if their penances were not inspired by God, not movements of grace, how did they produce the effect they seem to have produced? It would be contrary to the evidence to say that the Saints became Saints in spite of their penances rather than (in part, at least) because of them. They became Saints in spite of their faults, but their penances show all the signs of having helped them along the way. What is the explanation of this?

The explanation is that the extremes of penance which we find in the Saints were not directly inspired by grace, but indirectly were the result of grace. The Saints received graces in their hearts too strong for them to hold there. They had to give expression somehow, someway, to the intensity of what they were receiving. The love, the sorrow, the desires in their hearts moved them to give passionate expression through their bodies, in their flesh, to the intensity of what they were experiencing in their souls. They allowed the grace they had received to express itself in and through their natures. And having activated nature in the expression of grace, they found that nature sometimes continued with an inertia of its own. This momentum of nature once excited in the expression of its love sometimes carried them into excess. St. Ignatius of Loyola almost killed himself, beating himself on the breast with a rock. He was picked up unconscious by friends and nursed back to health. God did not inspire Ignatius to pick up the rock; but God inspired the passion that led Ignatius to pick up the rock.

We can admire the graces, and the human passion inspired by those graces, which led the Saints into excess. But we cannot imitate the excesses themselves, because to "imitate" implies a cold, rational decision to reproduce an action that was in its original spontaneity the result of a flaming, uncalculating love. And if the action was in itself contrary to reason, it cannot legitimately be the object of a deliberate, rational choice.

Physical penances, however, can be an object of rational choice, if guided by prudence and moderation, and engaged in for the purpose of expressing passionate love for Christ. It should be obvious that the guidance of an experienced spiritual director is important here, because penance — or any other act, religious or not, that involves the emotions and body of man — is capable of taking directions that are more of nature than of grace.[12]

Practicalities are not passion

Just about everything one does in the celibate life might be called a physical expression of love for Christ, from living a real, material poverty to doing one's work each day. In this celibacy does not differ from marriage, where the physical expression of love is not limited to sexual relations either, but should be the reality of every action of one's life. But it really is not enough to express love through all of those things which, for practical purposes of their own, must get done from day to day, and which one does generously out of love for one's spouse. The very fact that such things as cooking, teaching, studying, nursing the sick have an immediate, practical value that would justify — or even require — one's doing them with or without the motivation of love for one's spouse detracts in some way from their pure unambiguity as symbolic gestures of love. A child in a hospital might complain, for example, that his parents did not love him if they did not visit him. Even though his parents provided everything possible for his cure, from twenty-four hour private-duty nurses to daily shipments of toys, this would mean nothing if they did not visit him. The visit is necessary precisely because it is unnecessary. A visit has no practical purpose; and therefore it can only be the expression of love.

---

[12] See St. JOHN OF THE CROSS, *Dark Night of the Soul*, Book 1, ch. 6, paragraphs 1-2 (in E. A. Peers, Image Books, 1959, pp. 53-55). See also DUBARLE, O.P., "Anthropological Factors Conditioning Acts of Penance" in *Christian Asceticism and Modern Man*, tr. Walter Mitchell, Philosophical Library, New York, 1955, pp. 202-205.

To sit up all night by the bedside of a sick child, especially if one knows nothing of nursing care and a private-duty nurse is already on hand, is "foolishness" by the measure of practicality. For that very reason it is more important, in terms of expressing love, than anything practical one might do. It is true that symbolic gestures cannot replace practical responses to another's needs. But cold, practical ministration to another will never replace symbolic gestures of love either. This is why it reveals a basic misunderstanding of the very nature of penance when someone says, "My penance is my work"; or "Just living in this community is penance enough for me". The right word to use here would not be "penance" but "mortification", or the practical subordination of nature to the demands of reason and grace. To work at subduing one's selfishness is a constant offering and gift of oneself to God, and it was the practice of the Saints (such as St. John Berchmans, for example, who exclaimed, "My greatest mortification is living the life of the community!"). But to do, and do faithfully, what one is obliged to do by the circumstances of one's life — perseveringly accomplishing one's work, responding generously to the importunities and foibles of the neighbor, etc. — is not penance as we have described it here. It is simply practical Christian living. And when one responds perfectly to all that life's circumstances demand, the demands of love are still not satisfied. One can only say "I am a servant" — and a "useless servant" at that — so long as one's service is not salted with the foolishness of passionate love.

Faithful Christian living lacks the element of passion required for us to keep Christ's love in perspective. Without moments of passionate response to Him we begin to forget the immensity and passion of His love and desire for us. We unconsciously begin to think that all God really asks of us is that faithful service which He himself described as the life of an unprofitable servant: "When you have done all you have been commanded to do, say 'We are useless servants. We have done no more than our duty.'" (Luke 17: 10). We think it is not important to Him what we do "on our own time", after the hours of work or community obligations are over. We lose our realization of how much He is concerned, how much He cares, about every detail and expression of our being. We fall into the error of St. Teresa's confessors, who told her that things she thought were indelicacies toward God were not sins, or at least of no importance. This amounted to saying that God did not love Teresa as much as Teresa loved God — because God apparently was not as interested in receiving everything from her as she was in giving everything to Him. Her confessors should have encouraged her (as it seems one of her confessors subsequently did), to profess passionately to God in penance her regret at having denied Him anything, her determination to let Him reign in her flesh without restraint.[13]

Passion is needed

A religious life without moments of passionate expression of love to God would be like married life without intercourse. Married couples tell me that intercourse is a "cement", it holds them together. I never understood the real function of intercourse in marriage until a beautiful Christian wife gave a talk on marriage for me during a retreat to university

[13] See St. Teresa's *Life*, ch. 5, par 11 (E. A. PEERS, *The Autobiography of St. Teresa of Avila*, Image Books, 1960, p. 85), and ch. 24, par. 3 (Peers, p. 229). See also *Interior Castle*, "Third Mansions", ch. 2, par. 7 (Peers, Image Books, 1961, p. 65): The "eminently reasonable" religious of the Third Mansions is not about to kill herself with penance. Her penances are as "carefully ordered" as the rest of her life.

students. She told the students that intercourse was for her like a miracle of God. When she and her husband would get into fights that ended in days of not speaking to one another, they would finally have intercourse and all would be forgotten. For herself, she said, who carried grudges for years, this was a miracle. But to my mind at the time, sitting there analyzing everything she said through the rational categories I had been trained in, her story was illogical. Fights are caused by objective disagreements: one wants the window up, the other wants the window down, and that's an objective fact. Having intercourse — a physical, emotional experience as I understood it at the time — does not change facts. The window would still be up or down. What I failed to understand was the element of perspective. It is true that intercourse does not change the reality; but it puts the reality into perspective. Through the passionate, physical gift of themselves to each other in love, the reality of a couple's love and commitment to one another becomes vivid to them both. They become aware of their depths. In the light of this renewed awareness, the problem of the window just loses its importance. It is still a problem but an insignificant one. In the light of the love they have for each other, who cares about the window?

I began to understand through this the significance of the Passion of Christ in Christian spirituality. There are times when injustice is objectively done; when one is hurt, rejected in fact and not just in appearance; when one is wronged. For me — for all of us, I suppose — it simply seems beyond the nature of man to be able to really forgive such things. To forgive in the sense of not wishing to do the other harm in return, yes. But to forgive and forget — to really forgive, which means to accept to have again with that person the *same relationship one had before,* this seems simply impossible. And then we contemplate Christ in His Passion. In the light of the immensity of His love and suffering, the injustices to ourselves do not seem any less unjust; they just seem less important. The reality of His love becomes more to us than the reality of our own pain. And then we are able to forgive without bitterness or conditions, from the heart.

This is what any passionate experience of love does for our lives; it puts everything else in perspective. Two friends quarrelling as they walked, who suddenly were witnesses to a tragic accident, would simply forget their quarrel in their awareness of and proximity to real tragedy and pain.

The destructiveness of "reasonable service"

One of the worst mistakes we can make in religious communities is to hold up "reasonable service" as our norm. Reasonable service, as I use the expression here, is not the phrase of St. Paul in Romans 12: 1, but is a synonym for tepidity. It is that perfectly well-ordered life, that high level of mediocrity, that St. Teresa describes as the "Third Mansions" of *The Interior Castle*. A religious feels the desire to give and give passionately to Christ. We encourage him to keep the Rule, follow the community, do his work, and be satisfied. We invite him to be "neither hot nor cold" so that God will vomit him out of His mouth — if he doesn't vomit God first. And then we wonder why, a few years later, he is a sour, dissatisfied man, or a restless, unhappy woman — or has simply left religious life for a more challenging relationship in marriage. The "Third Mansions" religious is a person who has mastered the moral virtues; who is able to keep the Law. This is the "good religious", than whom there is nothing more dangerous in religious life. The "good religious" has the respect of the community, because there are no discrediting weaknesses or failings in his life or in hers. The "good priest", the "good nun" leads an ordered life, works and prays on schedule, and knows how to get along with superiors or with those under him if he is in command. He is a good administrator, an efficient worker. He is usually restrained but articulate in community meetings. And every time a vision of faith, an inspiration of passionate response to Christ is proposed for community action, the "good religious" takes it apart piece by piece with cold, well-ordered logic. He is the destruction of religious life because he is the antithesis of passion. Celibacy without passion is bachelorhood at its worst, the functionalism of a career woman who has decided to live for things instead of for people. This person uses logic as a screen. He, or she, knows how to put the passion of others in its place, and does it with a political sang-froid that keeps his own position from ever coming under direct attack. Of this person St. Teresa says there is no danger he will ever kill himself by penance. And in community he will destroy the spirit of penance in others until they die. He will not leave them the passion they need to live.[14]

"There has got to be something more"

There is a movie called "Ryan's Daughter", in which a young Irish girl marries a schoolteacher who has all the qualities of an ideal husband except one: he lacks passion. In what, for me, is the key scene of the movie the girl is walking on the beach one day when she meets the old pastor who married them. He knows that something is wrong, and begins to tell her

[14] *Interior Castle*, "Third Mansions". ch. 2, parag. 7 (Peers, Image Books, 1961, p. 65).

what a fine man she has: steady, dependable, kind, upright, etc. She agrees with all he says but adds, insisting, "Father, there has got to be something more!" "There is nothing more," he answers. And he slaps her. He slaps her because he knows only too well that there is in fact something more, and that if she keeps looking for it, it will lead to ruin, which is exactly what happens. She finds an English officer who has nothing to offer but passion, and everything builds to disaster.

In religious life one meets "Ryan's daughter" every day. A nun (or a brother or priest) is dissatisfied — not because she is doing everything wrong, but because she is doing everything right, and is not finding what she expected. "There has got to be something more!" she is crying out to her community. And the community's answer is to slap her down. It is her community's insistence that their own mediocrity is the most one can expect of religious life that is her principal cause for despair.

The life of every religious must include enough love-inspired "foolishness" for the religious to remain aware of what he or she is — a person caught up in a relationship of passionate love and dedication to God through Jesus Christ. The symbolic gestures of love become passionate gestures from the moment that they can have no other justification or intelligibility except as uncalculating gestures of love. They are not contrary to reason but they go beyond reason. They are simply beyond comprehension to common sense. They cannot defend themselves in the forum of public debate. But they are the gestures love lives on.

Celibacy is the risk of spousal love

We have been trying to explain that the vow of celibacy establishes us in a real relationship of spousal commitment toward Jesus Christ in this life. It is a relationship made real through a concrete stance of renunciation toward marriage, one of the fundamental realities of human life on this earth. It is a real-symbolic gesture that expresses radical response to God, because the "stuff" of its expression is a real renunciation of something that reaches down to the very roots of a person's being in this world: one's power of sexual expression and procreation. This makes it a radical human act. And it is an unambiguous expression and experience of faith, hope, and love toward Jesus Christ, because it cannot be explained in any intelligible or justifying way except as a response to His word in the Gospel. Through our real-symbolic response to His word in celibacy, Jesus becomes real to us in a new way. By "taking Him for real" in actual fact, in the reality of a radical life-option, we both express and experience the truth of his reality to us.

We say that, objectively, religious celibacy is not intelligible or justifiable except as a response of faith to the Gospel. Could it be explained *subjectively,* in the life of this or that particular person, by other factors and motivations? Could it be that an individual religious may have chosen celibacy out of fear of marriage? Or because some work or community in the Church attracted him or her so much that he was willing to forego marriage in order to join this particular group of people? Or could one just be avoiding the risks and responsibilities of life in this world?

All this is possible, of course. There is no way to claim infaillibility about one's motivation. Who knows what the unconscious may cough up some day? But a person can have *moral* certitude about the motivation of a particular choice. Moral certitude is defined as that required for a serious moral act. It can also be the level of certitude that *obliges* us to decide in a particular case, when to insist on more evidence would amount to a refusal of the risk and responsibility of moral choice. Man's life is decisions, and they usually involve some risk. The very soul of a faith-decision is to risk everything one has, one's very life, on the *possibility* that Christ might be calling us to come to Him walking on the waters. All who followed Him in faith — Abraham, the Magi, Peter jumping out of the boat — knew that if the voice summoning them was not really God's they would lose their lives. But there was no other way to find out if it was God's than to follow it. Nothing was more illogical than Peter's challenge to the one he thought might be a ghost, "Lord, if it is you, call me to come to you walking on the water." If it had been a ghost intent on Peter's death, the answer would have been "Come!" And Peter would most probably have drowned. But when Peter felt himself summoned in answer to a prayer he addressed to God, he jumped. It was not contrary to logic: the voice could have been Christ's; there is reason to believe God will not let a man be deceived acting purely out of faith and hope and love. But the leap was a leap of faith, risking everything in trust. In that moment of leap, Peter knew that Christ was *worth* the risk of his life to him. Whether the voice was a ghost or not, he knew that Jesus was the only reality in his life.

PART THREE

COMMUNITY LIVING

CHAPTER SEVEN

The Help and Hindrance of Community Living

One of the greatest helps to living the vows — and one of the greatest hindrances — is community life. Except for hermits, whose status is receiving explicit, juridical recognition today, religious are understood to be people who live in community. Is this just by chance?

No, there are objective reasons why religious life calls for community. It is not our purpose to go into all of them here. Interested readers could study the motives that produced the transition from anchoritic (eremetical) life in the desert to cenobitic (community) life in monasteries in the time of Saint Basil and Saint Benedict. It was recognized then that a religious living by himself is subject to special dangers of illusion, subjectivism, unreality, selfishness, or aimless drifting that life in community and under spiritual government, can counteract.[1]

In our day emphasis is laid on community living as representative of the communal reality of the Church: communities stand out as "mini-Churches". Religious houses should be examples and proof of the power of the Spirit to unify hearts in faith and in love. They should be proclamations of the Christian

---

[1] Cf. *The Holy Rule* of Saint Benedict, chapter 1.

commitment to universal love. These goals, while perfectly valid for religious communities, are really goals for any Christian community; parishes, for example. But since authentic Christian community has become such a rarity in the Church today — a deficiency that has only just begun to be recognized and remedied — there is a tendency to make these goals specific to religious communities by default.[2]

Without denying any of these values, I would like to propose here that the fundamental purpose of religious community is to create an *environment of communal faith-expression* according to the spirit of the three vows. The purpose for this is *witness* and *mutual support.*

Together we stand — divided we fall

There is a sense in which the whole is much greater than the sum of its parts. If you have three logs burning in a fireplace and you separate them, they will all grow cold and their fire will die out. Put them together and they will all burn with new life — and give warmth to the whole house. This is the way it is with faith-communities: the faith, hope, and love of individuals living in isolation inclines to grow cold; give those same individuals a community of shared faith, hope, and love, and they take on new life. Likewise, the witness of a lone individual living the Christian life, inspiring as it is, is liable to be confused with his own talents and gifts: he stands out as an extraordinary person. But the fact of a whole community living by Christian principles is a witness to the appeal of the Gospel and the power of the Spirit

---

[2] See Father Jerome MURPHY-O'CONNOR, O.P., "What is Religious Life? — ask the Scriptures", in *Supplement to Doctrine and Life,* May/June, 1973.

as such. It is Christianity that stands out and not just an extraordinary human being who happens to be a Christian.

To say that religious need the mutual support of community living is not to say that religious are weak people, psychologically dependent on others, unable to stand on their own two feet. It is probably true that man needs societal support even on the psychological level, just to live by sound rational principles. The higher his vision and ideals, the more support he will need to persevere in living them, I would suppose. This may not be true of certain, exceptional people — there is a saying that "the eagle flies alone" — but it is true for men taken as a whole. But even if it were not true on the human, psychological, rational level, nevertheless, when there is question of living a life of faith, the graced life, we are facing another picture. We are on a different level entirely. Where human, rational decisions can find an evident, visible support in the clarity of concrete reasons and obvious common sense, faith decisions cannot. Rational choices will be endowed with strength in the measure that the reasons supporting a choice are more and more evidently clear. And these reasons can be so clear that they leave a man no room for doubt. But faith-decisions are by definition without visible support. They are choices man makes on the evidence of God's word alone: God's word speaking to him through Scripture, God's word urging in his own heart. The grounds of faith are not visible, even though they are the deepest experience of a man's life. The fact that faith is the strongest, most certain light man can live by does not make it the most evident, clear, or visible light man can see.

In moments of consolation, which St. Ignatius defines as those moments when the truths of faith are able to inspire and motivate one psychologically, when all is clear and inviting that is illumined by the light of faith, in these moments it is easy to live — that is, to make one's choices — by faith. But in moments of desolation, when the truths of faith do not inspire or move one at all, when all is confused, dark, and meaningless, what has man got to fall back on?[3]

Making the reality of faith visible

In those moments the faith becomes visible in the humanity of others; it is the word of faith made flesh in my brother's life that supports me. What makes Christ visible when He is not visible to me, is the way that others are visibly responding to Him. His reality becomes visible through the fact that others are visibly taking Him for real. His presence appears through the visible recognition of His presence in the way the community acts.

The life of the community is, or should be, an external reflection of the vision of faith in my own heart, of the light I live by. When that light becomes dark within me, I can still see by the light that is shining from others. When the flame in my own heart seems to be dying out, the fervor of those around me keeps me burning until I can catch fire again. When I share my flame with others, and they with me, we enkindle each other's hearts to burn more brightly, and we keep the fire going until each one is totally consumed. That is why it is true to say that to express my faith in community is to store it for future use. I bank my light and warmth in others by expressing it to them, and then I draw upon it in my moments of need.

[3] St. IGNATIUS LOYOLA, *Spiritual Exercises*, "Rules for the Discernment of Spirits", paragraphs 316-317, (Chicago, Loyola University Press, 1951, p. 142).

Obscuring the reality of faith

The same metaphor, of logs in the fireplace, explains what happens when anyone in the community is not really giving himself to be enkindled and consumed by the Holy Spirit. Put damp wood or green wood on a fire and it smokes; it suffocates the flame of all; it takes away the very air the fire must breathe to stay alight; it blankets the light and covers everything with smoke and obscurity. One man, just living as if Jesus were not the most important reality in his life, does more to destroy the atmosphere of faith in a religious house than any amount of explicit sin and repentance. It is mediocrity, as an enduring state, and not the sins of a moment, that suffocates faith.

Vatican Council II says that the chastity of celibate religious "has stronger safeguards in a community where true fraternal love thrives among its members."[4] I used to think this just meant that if a religious does not find love at home he will go looking for it elsewhere. Now I think the doctrine expressed here is much deeper than that. If a religious does not find reflected in his community the *fruits* of a life of celibate loving — such as the love, the joy, the peace that are the fruits of the Holy Spirit — he will become disillusioned with celibacy as such. Religious life claims through its vow of celibacy to be centered on the person of Jesus Christ in love, and to give to all of its members the fruits of an authentic relationship of spousal love with God. If it reveals itself instead to be a breeding house for a closed-up spirit of narrow selfishness, and to produce petty, defensive people, then pretty soon the members are going to see themselves, not as community of celibates or virgins, but simply as a collection of bachelors and old maids.

4 "Decree on the Appropriate Renewal of Religious Life", paragraph 12, (Abbott, pp. 474-475).

Religious who do not love one another cannot be lovers of Christ. A celibacy that produces this kind of person cannot be worth the investment of one's life.

Likewise, when a religious community finds that it can discuss and come to agreement on common-sense, business-of-the-day issues, but cannot agree on — or perhaps even discuss — the deeper questions of the spiritual life, that community is in trouble. When communal decisions reflect respect and deference toward the demands of high-quality professional work, of enlightened political involvement, and of a sound psychology of personal freedom, for example, but reveal very little awareness of the demands of life in common in faith and prayer, then that community is basically just a club for professionally involved Christians. It is a sort of Catholic B.O.Q. (Bachelor Officers' Quarters) for dedicated militants. But it is not a community for religious to survive in.

The community's expression of itself

The tone of a community will reflect the inner reality of its members' lives. Some religious communities appear to be — and may well be in fact — nothing more than private, professional clubs; places where men or women dedicated to the same work can live together in a humanly supportive way. A tone of availability and easy camaraderie prevails in the house. The lifestyle is designed to facilitate the professional work of each member — and to leave each one the greatest possible freedom in every other respect. The community will probably have agreed on certain expressions of the Christianity proper to its own milieu. Whatever is best and most current in the Church in general will be recognized in some way in the communal expression of the group. The recognition might be a token one, but it will be according to the guidelines laid down by the leaders of whatever movement is of current Christian concern. If banners are in, banners will be up. If lettuce is under boycott, lettuce will not appear on the table. The right books will be found on the shelves, the right clippings posted on the wall. In the struggle for social justice, the right heroes and villains will be applauded and booed. The community's actual involvement or sacrifice may be small, but it will be declaring itself on the proper side. There will be signs of identification with those movements, causes, or parties in the Church which the community finds itself in sympathy with. This is all very good, of course, provided it doesn't stop here.

The problem comes when in such communities the lifestyle itself appears to be basically determined just by the professional work and interests of its members. These interests will include, of course, their professional interests as Christians of a particular apostolic involvement, intellectual stratum, or social milieu. Those apostolically involved with the rich will reflect in their lifestyle identification with the rich. Those apostolically involved with the poor will reflect in their lifestyle identification with the poor. The community will be visibly identified with certain groups or movements in the Church, according to its professional and apostolic interest. This is good in the measure that the movements themselves are good. But what will not be visible is any particular identification of the community with the specifically Christian spirit of faith, any unmistakable devotion toward the person of Jesus Christ as such. There will not be any explicit, radical, unambiguous centering of the hearts of all the members on the person of Jesus Christ.

The ambiguity of cultural movements

Can one be centered on Christ without being identified with the direction the Church is taking in our day, and without adopting her concerns? Of course not. But can one be identified with certain authentic movements and directions of the Chruch in one's own time without being centered on Jesus Christ in faith? Yes, one can. And the reason for this is that the Church is concerned, and authentically concerned, about many things which do not require faith in Christ for their justification. One cannot be a Christian without concern for the poor. But one can have concern for the poor without being a Christian — without even being an anonymous Christian. To argue that just because one has fed the hungry or clothed the naked one will automatically be placed among the sheep on Judgment Day is to return to a literalism that is fundamentalism at its best and a more subtle form of Phariseeism at its worst. Works do not save without faith, any more than faith can be valid without works. To pour oneself out on obviously good causes, whether these be the education of the rich or the emancipation of the poor, can be a way of just not facing the question of whether one does or does not fundamentally believe in Jesus Christ.

In addition to the fact that one is not necessarily sure of believing in Christ just because one believes in Christian causes, there is the added question of just how Christian a given work or cause may be — not perhaps in its goals, but in the means adopted to achieve those goals. History is filled with examples of Christians acting in the name of Christ but in the spirit of the devil. Christians have celebrated the rites of Satan for centuries by persecuting the Jews in a grotesque mime of giving glory to Christ. The officers of the Inquisition cooperated with rack and fire in the Church's movement against heresy in the Middle Ages. The Crusaders carried war and bloodshed halfway across their world in response to a Christian concern of their day, often delivering the soul of Christ's people to the devil in order to liberate His

birthplace from the infidel. And even in our day we
see Christian monks — Catholic vs. Orthodox —
battling with sticks in the very sanctuaries of the Holy
Land, quarrelling like tragic children over whose turn
it is to celebrate Mass next! Christian priests and
bishops encouraged Hitler in his war — a war we
must acknowledge as having been in some degree
"our war", and our guilt, by that very fact. What war
has not found Christians exhorting the troops to fight
and kill gallantly in the name of God? In the light
of these obvious examples from the past, are we so
naive as to think that our own popular enthusiasms
are immune from infection? Have we nothing to fear
from the violence of our pacifism, the prejudice of our
tolerance, the partiality of our concern for justice in
the world? There is simply no security in following
any movement in the Church or in the world unless
at the same time we can have some assurance, through
intimacy with the Spirit of Christ Himself, that we are
also following the direction and the spirit of His
Heart: merciful, compassionate, forgiving, humble,
and kind. Jesus showed love, not by crucifying others,
but by offering Himself for crucifixion. In the last
analysis, the justice of our causes will be measured
by the love in our hearts.

Acknowledging Christ together

It is easier to recognize the intramundane justice
of a Christian cause and fight for it through the use
of worldly power than it is to recognize the reality of
Christ Himself as person in our midst and to embrace
His means for the redemption of the world. In the
type of religious community we are criticizing here,
we often find it easier to enlist community support for
something obvious, like a crusade, than to unite the
community in an unambiguous expression of faith in
the invisible presence of Christ really working among

us. I am speaking here of deeply personal expressions, of course, not of pious devotions. Religious communities will easily accept some formalized expression of prayer together, something that allows for an all-but-neutral participation of the members, that does not explicitly engage the heart of each one. But ask religious to declare in personal, spontaneous ways together their faith and love for Jesus Christ, and the demurring murmur begins. Why is this? Why do we not want to be demonstrative about our faith in public, even in the very private public of our own religious houses? Is this really just a cultural hangup, or is there a deep hesitancy and ambiguity on the level of faith itself underlying the resistance we experience?

Faith expression a threat to mediocrity

Some religious resent any invitation to declare aloud their response to a reading from the word of God in Scripture. Some resist any visible expression of poverty in the house — not because they are all that attached to things, but because the very expression of faith on this level troubles their waters, suggests the presence of wind and waves and waiting depths outside the complacent little inlet in which they had thought to finish out their days. Others resent any gesture that would imply that obedience should be for them anything more than good, commonsense, communal decision-making — which they accept to call "discernment" if that pleases the worried, so long as the ultimate decision is based on the common denominator of consent. Obedience for them is primarily *doing* what makes sense, with personal agreement or disagreement on rational grounds. It is not essentially *believing* in the action of Jesus Christ. For these persons any situating of obedience on the level of faith that goes beyond mere words and phrases is upsetting.

In short, many religious get itchy when anything or anyone in the house reminds them too explicitly that professional work and Christian comradeship are not really what their life is all about. These people are uncomfortable with the faith; uncertain when they look for it deeply within themselves, uneasy when called upon to express it in personal ways. These are the "good religious" of reasonable, well-ordered lives. The very reasonableness of their lives makes them the most dangerous force religious community has to contend with. About them St. Teresa of Avila says that any religious who wants to follow his vocation authentically will have more to fear from the religious in his own house than from all the devils in Hell.[5]

Authentic religious community will express many things in its life, many different values. But above all it must express an explicit centering of faith, hope, and love on the person of the Lord. It does this on a structural level through visibly, explicitly, tangibly living the religious vows. Prayer must be a visible value in the house. Poverty must be a daily experience. Obedience must be an expressed reality. The community must be an environment in which all of the members express unambiguously to one another, in a language of action that leaves no doubt about its grace-inspired origin or direction, the place of the person of Jesus Christ in their lives. And the love that is expressed toward the Lord must be a love that does justice to what He is. It must be a passionate love. It must be a love that justifies the degree of sacrifice inherent in the celibate commitment.

[5] *Life*, chapter 7, paragraphs 4-5, (PEERS, Image Books Edition, 1960, p. 98-99).

If anyone loves the Lord but is ashamed to acknowledge Him in explicit, unblushing ways, that person should not be acknowledged as a disciple of Jesus Christ, much less as a disciple who has "left all things" to follow Him. We are not speaking here of gushy or sentimental testimonials, or of self-conscious little pieties that make everyone else feel like going home and going to bed. We are speaking of the freedom of adult persons, whose whole life is Jesus Christ, and who are not ashamed to speak of Him, in word and in action, in private and in public, through every detail of their life-style, individual or communal, without blushing before anybody. Such persons cannot play down their relationship with Christ without minting counterfeit images of the very persons that they are. The only artificiality they can conceive of is to hide the fact that Jesus Christ is passionately their All.

When such persons live together in community, they will communicate fire to one another. Their community will be good ground, in which the seed of life will grow. They will become a tree and the birds of the air will come to dwell in their branches.

CHAPTER EIGHT

The Uncommon Unity of Community

Is it possible to describe a little more in depth the nature of religious community and the way to achieve it?

Religious community must exist on three levels: it must be interpersonal first of all; it must be Christian; finally, it must be community according to the particular way of responding to the Gospel that is the way of life of a specific religious institute.

Interpersonal community

For community among human beings to be truly interpersonal, it must be a common unity on the level of *freedom*. When we use the term "interpersonal relationships" the image that sometimes comes to mind is that of two persons eyeball to eyeball sitting in a darkened booth over a glass of beer. Or the term might evoke associations of sensibility sessions or of communal sharing on a deeply-felt, emotional level. These images are misleading. No sharing of one's *thoughts* or *feelings* with another is interpersonal in itself. To share one's feelings with another is to present to that other the unfree workings of one's nature as a psychological mechanism. When you know another's feelings, it is precisely that other *not* as person that you know. True personhood exists only on the level of freedom; and therefore, until you know another precisely on the level of his free responses you do not know him as a person. That is why the analysis of another's psychological drives can never tell you anything at all about him as a person. Such analysis can only reveal the presence of certain factors that might — or might not — be the true motivation of his free, personal decisions. You know him as person only when you know how his *freedom* is acting in the context of his emotional drives.

Likewise, to share one's thought with another is to share with him yourself precisely as affected by objective, external reality. What a man thinks is determined, not by himself, but by the facts of reality outside of himself as he perceives it. It is true, of course, that a great deal of subjectivity enters into what we think, and into what we choose or decide to believe. But when one is sharing specifically on the intellectual level, one is trying to share oneself precisely as reflecting the truth of outside reality, not as revealing the secret of one's own free response to that reality. In intellectual discussions one tries to leave the personal, the free elements out; or to allow for them and to discount them as subjective responses distorting one's pure receptivity to objective truth.

It is only when we share with another the reality of our free, personal choices — our commitments — that we share ourselves as persons. And it is only through commitments that truly interpersonal relationships exist. For example, what is truly interpersonal about the fact of sharing our feelings with another is not that fact itself, but the *act,* the free choice we make to commit something of ourselves into another's hands, to make ourselves vulnerable to him, by sharing what is going on inside of us. In this case the commitment may be a very passing thing, hardly up to the real meaning of the word "commitment", and the duration of the relationship very brief. Or we might take an enduring stance of love toward another, make a real commitment to him, and then our relationship with him is a lasting thing, a part of our personal existence.

When we speak of "community" on the inter-personal level, we mean a common unity on the level of commitments. A group of people are committed to each other in specific ways. Or they are committed together to a common ideal or purpose. When some-one recognizes in another a commitment to the same ideal or purpose that he himself is committed to, there is a realization of a *common unity* that exists between them on the level of person. When people commit themselves to working *together* for this purpose, or to giving mutual *support* to each other in the embodiment of their common ideal, then they become a *com-munity*. Their common unity has taken the form of a communal commitment — both to the ideal, and to one another as committed to attaining it. Then there is a real, and a stable, interpersonal relationship between them.

Christian community

A *Christian* community is obviously a group of people committed to helping each other live in re-sponse to the reality of Jesus Christ. For any real community to exist among Christians, they must know each other as *persons responding to Christ*. I do not mean that they must have an intimate know-ledge of each individual's history, ideas, and emotions. But they must know in some way that each individual in the community has taken a personal, a free stance of faith, hope, and love toward Jesus Christ; that each one's faith, and each one's commitment is real. One way to come to such a realization is for each member

of the community to give his testimony, to tell how
he came to believe, or what his experience of Christ
has been. The most convincing way is for each person
to live in a way that simply would not make sense if
he were not a follower of Jesus Christ. But *expression*
must be given to one's commitment, and the expression must be understood — it must be "read" —
by others before community can exist. There are
many ways people can let each other realize that
they believe in Christ. The important thing is that
the realization should take place, for this is what
makes the reality of Christian community exist
(*exsistere*: "stand out") as truth and being to be recognized.

Religious community

A *religious* community is a group of persons
committed to responding to the Gospel in a particular
— and optional — way together. The commitments
that make up the interpersonal bond of a religious
community cannot be *deduced* from the Gospel as
necessary, logical conclusions that follow from the
teaching of Jesus Christ. If religious life could be so
deduced from the Gospel, it would be a logical conclusion for every Christian, and anyone who wanted
to be a perfect disciple of Jesus would have to become
a religious. There was in the past a tendency to understand religious life in precisely this way: non-
religious were Christians who engaged themselves only
to follow the *commandments* of Christ, those things
Jesus taught we *must* do. Religious were Christians
who accepted to follow Christ's *counsels* as well, the
things He *invited* and urged men to do; invited, at
least, all those whom He called to be "perfect". This
understanding of religious life coincided with a
teaching on the vows that presented them as *removing*

obstacles to freedom, as taking away attachments that prevented men from being holy.[1]

Any understanding of the vows that distinguishes the life of religious from that of secular Christians only in terms of a "more" — a more logical, more complete, or more generous following of the Gospel — is in contradiction with the teaching of the Church today. Vatican II's Constitution on the Church teaches that "it is evident to everyone that all the faithful of Christ of whatever rank or status are called to the fullness of the Christian life and to the perfection of charity."[2] Hence religious life cannot be just a logical conclusion from the Gospel that imposes itself on anyone who truly desires to be perfect in response to the teaching of Christ.

Religious life — and even more so the religious life proper to a particular religious order or institute — is not so much a way of interpreting the Gospel as a way of responding to the Gospel. Someone called to be a founder looks at the Gospel and the Holy Spirit comes around behind him, as it were, and inspires him with a way of responding to what he sees. Those who join him or the community he founds are united, not just by the fact of responding to the Gospel together as Christians, but by the fact that they have received the grace to see and accept for themselves this particular way of responding to the reality and teachings of Jesus Christ.

What justifies the way of life of any religious congregation is not the fact that this particular way

---

[1] Cf. St. THOMAS AQUINAS, *Summa Theologica* II-II, Q. 186, art. 7; St. Ignatius Loyola, *Spiritual Exercises*, "Introduction to the Consideration of Different States of Life", par. 135, (Puhl, Loyola University Press edition, p. 59); Adolphe TANQUERAY, *The Spiritual Life*, Part I, ch. 3, art. 2, (Newman Press, 1930, p. 171).
[2] Chapter 5, par. 40, (Abbott, p. 67).

of life can be demonstrated as a logical conclusion from the Scriptures. It is justified by three things: First, by the fact that the way of life can be shown to be *inspired by the Scriptures,* to be "in tune" with the word of God, to be a way of embodying the spirit of the Gospel. Secondly, a particular way of life must have the *testimony of the Holy Spirit.* And this testimony is given through the fruits that it bears. If the founder's life is obviously holy, manifesting the presence and power of the Holy Spirit; if the experience of those who follow his vision is an experience of grace, of newer and deeper life in faith, hope, and love; and if the Christian people respond to the new community in a way that shows it to be productive of fruit apostolically, then all of this is evidence of the inspiration and power of the Spirit of God at work. Finally, the way of life must be *approved by the official teaching and governing authority in the Church.* This is the final seal on the orthodoxy of any person's vision of a way to respond to the Gospel. In giving such approval, the Church does not say this is the best or only way to respond to the Gospel; just that it is a valid way, and that anyone who responds this way will be responding in a way that is authentically Christian according to the Church's understanding of herself at that moment of her history.

The two meanings of "community"

On each of these three levels — interpersonal, Christian, and religious — the word "community" can mean two things, depending on the aspect of community one is immediately concerned with. Community can be a reality that I help create, to which I contribute; or community can be a milieu that re-creates me, something that supports me. In the first sense community challenges me to *love;* in the second it provides me with *friendship.*

The words "love" *(agape, amor)* and "friendship" *(phileia, amicitia)* have a long history in philosophical and theological writing, and much profundity has gone into the efforts to distinguish between them. We don't intend to dig so deeply here; just to turn over the surface soil of these concepts and see what easily comes to light.

The essential difference between love and friendship is that love is a free act whereas friendship is not. I can give love — to anyone I choose. But friendship is something that happens, and only between certain people. Love is free because its whole reality is commitment: if I commit myself to act toward another according to the terms of a certain relationship (parent, spouse, fellow countryman, etc.), then I love him in that relationship, and my love is authentic and real. It does not make any difference what I feel about him or experience when I am around him. Insofar as the nature of love as such is concerned, its reality is the reality of my commitment, nothing else. We quote St. Teresa of Avila again: "Love consists, not in the extent of our feelings of contentment *(gusto),* but in the firmness of our determination."[3]

But the reality we associate with friendship I am not free to command. Friends are able to relax with each other, to enjoy themselves together. They have a certain oneness of attitudes and values, a mutual understanding and acceptance of one another. There is an easiness in their relationship, an absence of strain. Love can be laborious; friendship is not. Friends are simply "at home" with one another. They like to be together. That is why it reposes and re-creates us to be with friends.

[3] *Interior Castle,* "Fourth Mansions", ch. 1, par. 7, (Peers, Image Books 1961, p. 76).

This reality of friendship depends on many factors not directly under man's control. People can be psychologically incompatible. They can have radically different attitudes and values, and be convinced of them. Their tastes can differ. Their previous histories may make it hard for them to communicate or accept one another. None of these obstacles can prevent people from *loving* each other, from making and living by commitments to each other. But these obstacles can prevent them from ever really relaxing or enjoying themselves together. They can be real obstacles to friendship.

From love to friendship

On the level of interpersonal relationship, community depends on the free commitments people choose to enter into with each other. Community as an interpersonal relationship is always within our power. This is community as *love*. But community as interpersonal *friendship* involves more than our persons, our freedom. To really find friendship with each other, we must already have, or manage to arrive at, a certain *co-naturality*. Our natures — the "givenness" of our being that is already there, molded ahead of time by forces not under our control — must in some way jibe or be brought to jibe and fit together. Interpersonal community, then, can have two meanings: as love it is an interpersonal relationship that depends only on the freedom of those involved. As friendship it is co-naturality, and this cannot be directly or immediately willed into existence.

We can say, then, as a general rule that *love* can be, and always should be, a reality in community; and that where people really love each other as they should, most frequently their love will *lead to friendship*. The friendship produced will be that which corresponds to the kind of love relationship that exists. Love for one's fellow countrymen, for example, is commitment to acting toward them according to the ideals, laws, and customs of one's own particular society or culture. Where all Canadians *act* in the way that Canadians (theoretically, at least) understand themselves to be committed to act they will feel "at home" in each other's presence. They will know what they can count on from each other, and what they need not fear; they will find it pleasant and helpful to live together in the same country or city. They will feel a certain bond of appreciation for each other just as fellow Canadians. They will communicate easily about things great and small: human freedom and hockey, equality and justice and the slang and fads of the day. Where *love* is a reality between countrymen, *friendship* between them — on a certain level, at least — will be a reality as well. But the common unity of friendship that exists will be only on the level of the common unity of love that is committed.

Achieving Christian community

In a *Christian community* people commit themselves to something more: to living and expressing the Gospel to one another. Those who do this in love will find themselves united in the "friendship of the faith". They may not be psychologically compatible as friends in the usual sense of the word. They may have different tastes, mannerisms that jar each other, disagreements about many things on the intellectual level. They may not mix well in social gatherings or work smoothly together in certain team situations. But when it comes to that which they have in common, their mutual commitment to responding to Christ in faith, they are able to relax and be themselves with one another. Here they understand and appreciate each other, and feel themselves to be understood and appreciated. Among themselves they find an atmosphere that allows them to discuss freely their experiences and aspirations of faith. They can pray easily in each other's company, both individually and communally. They re-create, restore, and confirm each other in response to Christ, in the life of Christian faith, hope, and love. They are grateful for each other because of the support and receptivity they find in the sharing and expressing of their life on its deepest level, the level of seeing and loving all things in the light of Jesus Christ.

But this friendship in the faith, this community of spiritual support and enjoyment, depends on each one's *loving* as he should. If anyone "breaks the bond of faith" by actions or expressions that are contrary to the common commitment to Christ, then malaise results in the community. People no longer feel certain of each other, no longer free to express themselves spiritually, no longer sure of the reception their self-expression will meet with. They close up, become protective of what is most deeply and vulnerably their own.

Even more destructive, perhaps, than actions directly and explicitly contrary to the faith are words or gestures that express a sophisticated disdain for simply spontaneity or devotional emotions as such. The sophisticate who makes a point of being always in control of himself denies implicitly the supremacy of God. Like King David's wife he scorns those who dance naked before the Ark of God. (2 Sam. 6: 20). His scorn can take the dance and the spontaneity out of a whole community as effectively as a blow to the stomach can stop a laugh. Who can freely be himself under the Kleig lights of a sneer?

As a matter of fact, in order to inhibit a person from expressing the love he has for God it is normally

enough just that nobody else expresses this love.
Newcomers to a community pick up a whole code
of implicit do's and don't's. The very "tone" of a
house is freeing or inhibiting. And this tone is determined above all by the self-expression of the people
already there. The more reserved and formal the tone
of the community's expression of itself to God, the
less encouraged anyone will be to treat God as someone worth getting excited about. (We are not speaking
here against solemn liturgical services, of course). If
devotion is never personally and spontaneously expressed, the implicit assumption will be that devotion
personal enough to be spontaneous or emotional in
its expression is somehow frowned upon; that God is
real enough to receive formal recognition, but not so
real that we should give spontaneous expression and
enthusiastic expression to what we say we believe
about him, in ways that leave no doubt about what
He really means to us. We like a certain amount of
ambiguity to hide behind. To declare ourselves is to
confront the reality — or unreality — of our love.

And so, in order to inhibit the free expression of
faith in others, it is really enough just not to express
faith freely yourself. That is why real faith communities make a point of giving expression to the faith,
the hope, the love that is within them, and of en-
couraging this expression in others.

Where authentic Christian love exists, a love that
wants each one to *esse et bene esse* in the words of
St. Augustine: to be all that one is and to become all
that one can become, the expression in personal and
spontaneous ways of each one's love for God will be
accepted as something to be taken for granted among
believers.

Not only this, but it will be taken for granted
that each one loves God or wants to love God
passionately. No other kind of love can truly

claim God as its object. But the reality of passionate love is that it is not steadfastly measured or reserved in its expression. And so, in a community that understands total love of God, there will be no value set on a sophisticated coolness of control in one's expression of devotion. There will be no value set on artificial sentimentality either. The community's devotion will ring true, deep, and authentic as a love that frankly and directly declares God to be the center and scope of each one's mind and will and heart.

The expression of a community's devotion takes place in non-verbal even more than in verbal ways. It is not so much what one says as the way one acts that reveals what God really means to a person. One's use of material things speaks. The time one gives to prayer speaks. So does everything else that is the visible extension or expression of one's personality. But the fact of accepting or not accepting to give verbal utterance to one's heart is also an *act* in itself. Words have very little value; but the free choice to express or not to express oneself in words is an action that speaks more eloquently than the words themselves. Hence Christian communities must not be inhibited in their speech any more than in their actions when it comes to proclaiming that God is everything to them.

Religious community as friendship

When we look at *religious community* the same truth appears. In the measure that religious live their love by keeping the commitments that bind them to one another, in that same measure they will grow into *friendship* with each other as well. For one thing (and this should be true of any Christian community), as their lifestyle helps them to grow toward union of mind and will and heart with Jesus Christ, they will grow toward this same union with each other in Him. In addition to this, by living the commitments proper to their own religious institute, they will grow in the spirit of their institute, the spirit that was the charism of their founder. In this way they will grow into unity and mutual understanding, not only in their common acceptance of the Gospel, but also in their particular way of responding to the Gospel as members of their own particular religious institute.

Need for expression and common language

We see immediately that in order for love and commitment to grow into friendship and the experience of community, it is absolutely essential that the commitment of all the members be *expressed,* and expressed in a language of *symbolic gestures* that everyone understands. A group of dedicated Christians living in the same building are not by that fact a Christian community. It is possible to have a house full of religious without having a religious house. For community to exist, people must *recognize* one another as committed to the same things. This means that everyone's commitment must be expressed, and expressed in language that is both understandable and credible to others. The clearest language, perhaps, is words. But this is also the language that is least credible. In the measure that words are not backed up by actions they lose their credibility. They are like so much paper money. Every time a community issues a communal statement of ideals and does not live by it, the community devaluates its own currency. Soon even the members of the community stop taking chapter decrees seriously or paying any attention to the letters that come out of the provincial's office, if these do not have any visible effect on the community's lifestyle.

The importance of symbols

The only language that is credible in itself is the language of actions, of real-symbolic gestures. We believe what people do. But the difficulty here is that sometimes we do not understand what they do. We know that every choice a person makes is an act of self-expression, but we do not always know what it is inside of a person that is finding expression in a particular action. Sometimes he does not know himself.

This is why symbols, and especially symbolic actions, are so important in community. It is our symbolic actions that back up the printed currency of our words. We are speaking here of real symbolic actions: actions that both express (are thus "symbols" of) our interior orientation, and whose expressive content is made up of real values (thus real-symbols). Actions that engage or invest our being, choices that speak by involving or risking things that are of real value to us: our possessions, our time, our friendships, our possibilities of achievement — these are the actions that express us real-symbolically. And these are the only clearly credible language through which the reality of a person's commitment is communicated to others.

How explain a phenomenon of our day which seems to contradict what we have just said? We have seen one community after another torn apart over what would appear to be very *un*real symbols, symbols which do not seem to involve any real value at all, or very little value at best. Priests' communities found themselves chin to chin with each other a few years ago over tiny details of liturgical observance at Mass. Sisters' communities were split right down the middle over the question of habit: long, short, or secular. Beards and long hair were able to cause so much disturbance in the ranks of the faithful that you would think growing hair were an unnatural act instead of the original design of the Creator.

Here we have to recognize a few facts of human nature. The first is that any deep interior change that takes place within a person will inevitably manifest itself in some external way. The second is that the person himself may not be aware of the change that has taken place within him until long after its external manifestation has become part of his life. And the third is that sometimes very deep interior changes can express themselves externally in minute ways that seem to have little importance in themselves.

Take beards for example. In itself, the choice to grow a beard or not to grow a beard involves no more real value than the price of razor blades and the time it takes to shave. It could very well be that a choice like this would be dictated by nothing else than an aesthetic judgment about how attractive one might look. It could be. It could also be, however, that in a given culture where beards just don't exist, the choice to grow one might express a very deep decision to break with the culture. And the person growing the beard might not have any idea that this is what he is expressing. He may grow the beard thinking consciously only of how he will look, and not even realize that at that point he has already begun in an unconscious or subconscious way to feel himself an outsider to society. His friends might recognize his real reason before he does.

I am not saying that a beard *necessarily* expresses any deep interior change. If it does express a change, I am not saying it necessarily expresses the particular possibility I have mentioned, an emancipation proclamation from society. And finally, if it expresses an interior change, I am not saying that this change is necessarily unconscious or unrecognized. I am only saying that a choice like this *might* be the sign of a deep inner re-orientation of one's life, and that the external sign *might* appear before the interior reality is recognized for what it is, even by the person concerned.

In religious communities, where we cast in with each other not only our working hours and their possibilities of achievement, but also the whole actuality of our lives and our means to personal fulfillment, it is obvious that any deep re-orientation in the life of any member is going to be of great concern to all other members. The re-orientation might be a cause for joy; as, for example, when someone experiences a deeper conversion to God. Or the re-orientation might be a cause for distress, as when someone begins to be drawn away from the ideals and purposes of the community. But worst of all, perhaps, is a re-orientation that everyone feels has taken place in some member's life, but which no one can identify. When we know that someone has changed, but we do not know in what direction, or what to expect from it, then we do not know how to react. We feel anxiety without being able to say what is actually threatening us, or whether there is in fact any real danger developing against our community life, or how great it is if so.

Let's take another example from our times: When a religious decides to adapt, to put aside, or to return to the religious habit, he or she should ask what this is *expressing* in his life, and what it expresses to his community (and to the larger community of the Church). Everyone knows that "the habit does not make the monk". But we should also be very deeply aware that the decision to wear, or to stop wearing a habit has, or might have, a great deal to say about what image of ourselves as religious we have accepted. The habit does not make the monk; but it may well express the image the monk has of himself. And this has a great deal to do with what the monk is going to be.[4]

Whether a religious should or should not wear a habit is not the issue here; what we are concerned with is that no one should naively assume that such a decision is unimportant. The decision to wear or not to wear a habit could be, and I think in our own day generally is, a decision that reflects a very deep interior personal choice about the position one will take regarding the very nature of religious life as such.

Sometimes a person's decision about the habit — as about other details of lifestyle — reflects, not a personal attitude regarding the nature of religious life, but a decision to leave one's attitude in the hands of others. Take a Sister, for example, who makes the change into secular clothes one day after being for a long time the only nun in her house still to wear the veil. To the best of her knowledge, nothing in her religious life changes as a result of changing her dress. In such a case the change might well reflect a decision, not necessarily explicit or conscious, to stick with her community regardless of what direction the community might take in religious life. Before she makes the decision she is perhaps hesitating about how much she can identify with her community in the direction they are taking. After the decision it is clear that she has cast in her lot with the community, for better or for worse. I have known cases where a decision about dress was followed almost immediately by an appointment as superior, indicating that the community too may have been hesitating, waiting to be sure whose drum the Sister was going to march to before they invested her with power.

[4] Cf. Maxwell MALTZ, *Psycho-Cybernetics*, New York (Prentice Hall, 1960, Pocket Books edition, 1970).

I used to muse over whether deviations from expected liturgical practice upset congregations more than the preaching of false doctrine would. For example, if a priest declaimed from the pulpit that all dancing was sinful, and that parents who allowed their children to dance were going to Hell, would people react with as many phone calls to the bishop as they would have in the early nineteen-sixties if the same priest had said Mass in English or given communion in the hand? I think not. And the reason is that people can cope with what they understand. If one knows a priest is preaching falsehood, especially a more conservative falsehood that hardly anyone will pay attention to anyway, one tends to let it pass. But if one does not know *what* the priest is expressing by some symbolic action, such as changing the language or ceremonies of the Mass, one tends to get very upset and begin calling for the forces of law and order, or asking an explanation from authority.

It is not our purpose here to pass a value judgment on these human reactions. We just want to recognize them insofar as they are facts, and allow for them when we accept the responsibility of forming or fostering community among people.

What is essential is that each member of the community — and the community as a group — recognize the force of symbolic actions, and that each person take care to clarify, both to himself and to others, the origin and intention of every change in the actions that express his heart and soul; especially in the measure that these changes affect the communal commitment he has with other people.

Lines of communication

Communities live by mutuality. Communication is their lifeblood. And therefore effective language, both verbal and non-verbal, is as important to community living as arteries are to the body. When a community's language becomes encumbered with dead forms of expression, coated up with encrustations from the past, that community is suffering from hardening of the arteries. The passages of communication are blocked, and nothing can get through. Decline is immediate, and death just a matter of time.

For religious communities to remain vital, the self-expression of the members to one another must be clear and convincing on three levels of communication: First, the members must communicate real, personally-owned attitudes and commitments to one another. Their community must be interpersonal. Secondly, the members must communicate authentic response to the Gospel of Jesus Christ. Their community must be Christian. Finally, the members must communicate real understanding and acceptance of the vision that unites them as a religious institute. Their community must be religious. Their lifestyle must express a common commitment both to the specific way of responding to the Gospel that is characteristic of religious life as such, and to the particular way of responding within religious life that is the charismatic legacy of their founder.[5]

All three of these must go together. If external forms express true Christianity and the spirit of the institute, but for any reason have lost their credibility as true expressions of each person's inner conviction and commitment, then the religious community will be merely formalistic, a shell without life inside. It is

[5] On the need to agree on specific, and optional, details of lifestyle in order to express the common vision and commitment of religious community, see my article "The Problem of Religious Community Today," *Sisters Today*, Vol. 47, No. 5 (November, 1975), pp. 129-137.

important that something communicate to all the members the real, personal involvement and self-expression of each person who participates in the community's forms of communal self-expression. This means that no renewal of community life or spirit is possible without both the fact and the evidence of a corresponding renewal of spirit within the heart of each member. Renewal begins with individual conversions openly expressed.

Likewise the self-expression of the community must be authentically Christian, and recognized as such by all the members without questioning doubts. It is possible to *substitute* religious community for Christian community, in such a way that one focuses so narrowly on one's own way of responding to the Gospel that one loses sight of the Gospel itself to which one is supposed to be responding. Vatican II has seen fit to remind us that "since the fundamental norm of the religious life is a following of Christ as proposed by the gospel, such is to be regarded by all communities as their supreme law." As a way of returning to the authentic sources of all Christian life and spirituality, religious "should take the sacred Scriptures in hand each day." The day a religious puts more emphasis on his rules and constitutions than he does on the Scriptures, something has gone awry in his religious life.[6]

I'm afraid we may have been guilty in the past of reading our rules *instead* of the Scriptures. Certainly many of the things we did in the past in the name of our Rule we have since found, on closer examination, to be contrary to the principles of the Gospel. Because our houses were "religious houses" we could not offer ordinary Christian hospitality to people who came to

---

[6] "Decree on the Appropriate Renewal of Religious Life", paragraphs 2 and 6, (Abbott, pp. 468-471).

us for shelter. How many times did we sin against Christian charity, and even justice, on the excuse that we had a vow of poverty? There is no telling how many sins we went along with in the name of obedience — of a false concept of obedience, it is true, but the fact remains that we justified non-Christian actions on the grounds that our religious vows required it of us!

The guiding vision of the founder of any approved religious institute is a vision judged by the Church to be an authentic response to the Gospel. But the original embodiment of that vision in particular laws and practices is not guaranteed to retain the authenticity either of the Gospel or of the vision itself throughout all the changing circumstances of history. And therefore there must be a continuous re-evaluation of all the rules and practices of our religious life, not only in the light of Scripture but also in the light of "the original inspiration behind a given community", with an appropriate "adjustment of the community to the changed conditions of the times."[7]

Is there any practical way all this can be accomplished?

I would like to suggest just one. Let us presuppose that a community has already done its homework; that research projects have been carried out to determine more clearly the charism of the founder; that religious life has been studied in the light of Scripture and tradition; that meetings and workshops have been held and discussions engaged in. Let us suppose that the great majority of the community have returned to personal prayer on a regular basis; that they have made directed retreats and rediscovered the art of using spiritual direction. Let us also assume that

[7] *Ibid.*, p. 468.

people are still polarized as a result of new questions evoking a plurality of possible answers in the Church and in religious life today. But let us assume on the positive side that the intensity of battle has played itself out somewhat — that the warriors are all lying tired out on the ground, and the people who were shouting at each other a couple of years ago have shouted each other to a standstill and are willing to muse quietly now, without much hope of winning any debates. Let us also assume that people have been basically healed of the wounds inflicted on them in the past by a distorted understanding of religious life embodied in legalistic rigidities and anti-humanistic policies. Let us suppose that communities have tried beer and pretzels together, sensitivity sessions, business consultants, management techniques and group dynamics. Individuals have been allowed to "do their own thing", and groups to experiment with apartment living. Let us assume, in other words, that everything human has been accepted, respected, repaired, restored, and activated. What is still lacking to us? What more do we need to do?

Let's try praying together.

CHAPTER NINE

The "Contemplative Listening" of Communal Prayer

Let's start by saying that all community prayer is not communal praying. A group prayer can be just a collection of individuals saying their prayers out loud together at the same time. For prayer to be truly communal, the prayer of each individual must gain from the prayer of those around him. It must be different from private prayer by the addition of something other than just volume.

This can happen in many different ways. Reciting vocal prayers together can be truly communal praying. But we must take care to see that it is. Group recitation of the liturgical hours, for example, should add something not to be found in an individual's private reading of the Psalms, or else it is not truly communal praying.

In this chapter we want to discuss one particular way of praying together, one that is of special value and relevance — and perhaps even of necessity — in our times. We need to re-learn the art of *seeking God's will together in prayer.* It is through such seeking that communities discover and make real their oneness in the Lord.

Prayerful communal reflection is not something most communities are used to. We are accustomed to thinking of group prayer as the prayer of praise and petition, which it most frequently is. When there is question of meditating on God's word we spontaneously turn to private prayer. But it is possible for a group to seek light through God's word *together*, by communal reflection.

A communal reflection is not just an intellectual exercise. It does not mean that people just think and simultaneously share with each other what they are thinking about. For that kind of reflection it is better to meditate in private and come together later to share. Communal reflection is more of a *listening together*. It is a listening to God speaking through events or through His word as it is read; a listening at the same time to God speaking in one's own heart in response to what is presented; a listening to God speaking through one's brother who is sharing his own response to what is presented.

Contemplative listening

Praying together in this way could be described as "contemplative listening". I have been told that people listen to one another in different ways: curiously, critically, understandingly, contemplatively. It is this last way that interests us here. To listen to another contemplatively means that you listen with one ear to what your brother or sister is saying; with the other ear you listen to the reactions of your own heart; and while you are doing this you keep your eyes fixed on God, studying His face.

Sometimes what my brother says will excite a positive response in my heart, but one which I become ashamed of when I look at the face of Christ. For example, my brother may be reacting in a very emotional way to something, and his reaction may express perfectly my own instinctive reaction. And Christ may have to say to the two of us what He said to His disciples who wanted to call down fire and brimstone upon an unreceptive Samaritan town: "You do not know what spirit you are following." (Luke 9: 55). On other occasions I may react very negatively to what my brother says, rejecting his words immediately with feelings of opposition, hostility, or fear. Here again I look to the face of Christ to see whether I am rejecting my brother's orientation because I am a Christian or in spite of being a Christian. Not every approval of another's word is good; not every opposition is bad. Everything depends on the inspiration behind my reaction, on whether it is inspired by faith and love, or by selfishness and attachment to the spirit of this world.

Community and God's Word

Any community that is Christian should be able to pray together as naturally as men sit down to eat. No Christian should be threatened or uneasy at the prospect of facing God's word together with other Christians in an effort to bring God's light to bear on the way the community should live and work together. If anyone is threatened by this, what does this say about him or about the community?

If anyone is unwilling as a general rule to sit down together with his community and let the word of God confront the reality of his community's life, then that man should ask himself two questions: Has he really accepted Christianity unconditionally himself? Does he really believe his community is a Christian community?

It should not be shocking these days to suggest that many practising Catholics, and many priests and religious also, have never truly accepted Christianity, do not really believe in Jesus Christ. Oh, every practising Catholic believes in a verbal way in Christ;

everyone knows enough to affirm that He is true God and true man, the second Person of the Blessed Trinity made flesh for the redemption of the world. These words are easy to say. They cost nothing. That is why just to say them is not to have the slightest notion of whether one means them or not. The real test of whether one is a Christian in any personal way is to ask what *effect* the words and person of Jesus Christ are having on the day-to-day decisions that govern one's life. To believe in Christ is to accept Him as the Way, the Truth, and the Life — and this means really.

To accept Him as the Way means that one really does look to Him constantly for direction, that one follows Him as consciously as one would follow a path through the wilderness or navigate by the stars on the ocean. And one must do this in every decision that affects one's life.

To accept Him as the Truth means that one really tries to search out His attitudes and values, knowing that His truth is the only truth to live by. One wants to *know* how the teaching of Christ would apply to any given decision one is called upon to make in life. Not only does one want to know; one actively tries to know. One does not want to remain in complacent, untroubled ignorance, to be "let alone".

To believe that He is the Life is to be convinced that nothing outside of His Way or His Truth can really lead to fulfillment, to happiness, or to lasting good either for oneself or for the world. It is to believe that, whatever good we are seeking for ourselves or for the world, we will find it in Christ, in acting according to the mind and will of Christ, or we will not find it at all.

To be a Christian goes even further than this.

Confronting the Living God

To be a Christian means I accept relationship with the *living* God, and with the God who has *drawn near* to deal with me in human terms through Jesus Christ. It is not Christian to want to deal with God through the medium of the Law. A religion of law is a religion of contract. And the essence of a contract is to "freeze" freedom — to make my relationship with another impersonal. I deal with another through a set of objective, frozen commitments.

A contract replaces subjectivity with objectivity. The key word of a contract is "what": the contract tells me what I must do for the other, and what the other will do for me. Free choice comes into the making of a contract, and obviously one must continue freely to live up to its terms; but the free action of each party is limited to the "what" of the contract. Once the contract is made, I do not really deal with another's freedom anymore; the dealing has been done, it is just a question of carrying out what has been agreed on. And therefore, once I have made a contract with another, I cease to deal with that other precisely as a person. I now deal with the objective matter of the contract; I concentrate on *what* I must do, not on *whom* I am dealing with. My own person no longer comes into play either, except in the limited measure and manner required for me to do *what* I have promised. A contract reduces the relationship between persons to some "what" they have agreed on.

This is why it is so reassuring, so comfortable almost, to deal with God through the Law. The Law reduces my relationship with God, and limits His demands on me, to the observance of a certain number of specific, concrete things. Instead of facing the living God, infinite and unknowable, I face the cut-and-dried letter of the Law, predetermined and finite, quite comprehensible and exact. I have a religion to practise instead of a God to deal with. And those who embrace the religion of Law will hone its exactness to a fine edge. They will make laws to determine every possible interpretation of the Law, so that no one will ever have to make a decision, no one will ever have to relate for himself the objectivity of the Law to the subjective Person of God or take into consideration who God is, how He thinks and feels. No one will ever have to confront the Living God and take the responsibility of deciding for himself what might be according to His infinite mind and will. (No one will ever have to confront *himself,* either, and ask what his observance or interpretation of the Law really says about the orientation of his own deepest mind and will).

The religion of Law responds to the plea of the Jews when Moses came down from the mountain: "You speak to us, and we will listen; but let not God speak to us, or we shall die." (Exodus 20: 19 and Deuteronomy 5: 5, 22-27. Man fears encounter with the Living God; he fears he will not be equal to the demands for response that such an encounter lays on him. We know what happens when a lamp made for six volts is plugged into a hundred-and-ten-volt circuit: the light bulb shatters. We fear this for ourselves if we encounter the Being of God directly.

As long as God "kept His distance", remaining in the infinite separateness of His transcendence, there was small danger that any of us ordinary mortals would encounter Him as the Living God. Our system would not have to carry the load of responding to such a force of Truth and Love. That was reserved for the Saints and mystics, the specially-chosen who were strengthened and purified by God Himself for this purpose. But when Christ was born at Bethlehem God "drew near" to us all — not as if He reduced the distance quantitatively (God is equally present everywhere in this sense) but by reducing the qualitative distance between us: He became "like us in everything but sin"; that is He translated Himself into human terms: the Word of God became a human word, the Word made flesh.

From that moment any man could look on the face of the Living God and not die. The manner of God's revelation was not something so powerful, so supercharged with His own Being that we must shine instantly with the light and love of the mystics or burst our bulbs. God revealed Himself in a human way, and asked only that we respond to Him on the same terms. In Christ the grace of God expressed itself in human nature. In response to Christ we are only asked to let grace express itself in and through our own human natures in the same way that we have seen grace come to us through Jesus Christ.

Since we could not deal with God person-to-person as man to God, finite to Infinite, God became man. Now we can deal with God person-to-person on the level of man to man.

At this point the man who is sincere has no excuse. God does not ask us to bring our finitude into immediate contact with His Infinitude. He does not ask us to receive His current directly into our fragile globes. He asks us to deal with Him, to be "plugged in", so to speak, to His own reality as Person, but through a transformer. Through and in the humanity of Christ God's voltage is reduced to a measure we can handle. Through Christ we are in contact with the Living God, but in a manner adapted to our capacity for response. The voltage is reduced, but there is no break between us and the living power of God; our contact with God as Person is not broken; our religion is a live circuit.

The lure of a manageable system

In this context, to opt instead for a religion of Law is to reject the self-offering of the Living God. It is to ask for batteries in the place of live contact with the Power of God. This can be legitimate so long as man is unable to endure direct contact with God and no alternative to direct encounter with the Infinite is offered. But in Christ God offers Himself to us in human measure. And so, to live by the Law before Christ is one thing; to live by the Law after Christ is another. The Law as a preparation for Christ is pedagogy; the Law as a substitute for Christ is idolatry.

There can be no excuse, then, for turning away from the contact with the Person of God offered us in Jesus Christ; it can be nothing but a refusal of God Himself. And this is what the rejection of Christ by the Pharisees was: a refusal that was radical, that came from the very roots of their being; an insistence that they not be asked to come into immediate relationship with the Person of the living God, that they not be asked to respond as persons to His Person. "We have a Law, and according to that Law we want to live. Therefore, according to that Law He has to die."

Reducing God to roles

Isn't this the temptation of us all? Oh, we would all like some sort of immediate contact with the Person of God acting toward us in a limited way: God the Enlightener (giving light only in answer to the questions we ask Him, of course; not raising any issues of His own!); God the Healer (of the diseases we present to Him; not healing those things we would rather not be healed of or even have to admit as afflictions); God the Avenger (against others), God the Consoler, God the Wonder-worker, and so forth. We would all like God to come to us in these forms. But as soon as we say "in these forms" we have already excluded contact with the Person of God as such. For God as Person means God as He *is,* not God as acting toward us in some particular, limited way.

And so it is a contradiction in terms to ask for contact with God as Person, and at the same time to set any limits on what God might reveal to us, ask of us, or begin to do for us. To enter into relationship with God as He is, we must let Him be Himself.

Formalism as avoidance of God

This is what we fear, and what we refuse, whenever we cling to stereo-typed routines and patterns as the *only* way of expressing ourselves to God. To be afraid to sit down, alone or with others, and pray personally, spontaneously, in response to the word of God is really to be afraid of what God might say to us if we ever let Him speak outside of the script. We come with prepared speeches all written out, ready to listen to God's prepared speech that we have already read. We are terribly threatened if anyone departs from the text, because then God might say something unexpected too, and we might be called upon to respond to Him from the heart, as persons then and there, which is exactly what we are afraid to do, what we are trying to avoid.

Fear of communal reflection

We are afraid to do this alone, and we are even more afraid to do it with others. Alone we can exercise some control. Alone we can cheat and close our eyes to our cheating, or rule (as our own referees) that what we are doing is not really cheating at all.

Alone we are pretty certain (although God has a way of surprising us if we will accept to be silent!) that nothing really threatening will break through our defense mechanisms and walk naked into our consciousness. But with others no telling where the dialogue might go. No telling what someone is liable to say to God, that we will then be called upon to echo, or refuse to echo, in our own hearts. It is not a matter of being called upon to speak out loud to the group: it is a matter of certain things being brought up in God's presence that we would rather not be there for! — topics we have been trying to avoid with God, that no one else knows about, and that we ourselves have never consciously admitted we were suppressing. Then all of a sudden the coverings are stripped off, and there the issue stands, confronting us in the presence of God. It is a matter of certain rationalizations being stripped away in a communal reflection, leaving us with no other option than to say yes or no to the very heart of the matter, and to God Himself, asking us in person to respond to His call.

Fear a sign of attachment

If a community cannot reflect and pray together in this way, sitting down with an openness of spirit to let the word of God confront the reality of their lives; welcoming any suggestion from any member of the community as something to weigh contemplatively in their hearts in the presence of God; so that every member feels free to speak what is on his mind and in his heart without fear of defensiveness or attack from others — if a community cannot do this together, that community is afraid of encountering God. Another word for this fear is attachment: the community as a group, or members within it, are attached to something of this world that they do not intend to let go of even in response to the voice of God. Such a community is not really together in order to accept and follow Jesus Christ as the Way, the Truth, and the Life. They are clinging to their own way and truth as to the path they want to follow. Life for them is not Jesus Christ. Life for them is to live by the plans and specifications they have already accepted. They are anxious about many things, but they are not particularly anxious about the will of God. They have a Law, and according to that Law they want to live. They are familiar with its demands, comfortable with what it requires of them. Into such a circle Jesus Christ can only enter as an intruder. If He does, then according to their Law He has to die.

Communal reflection in religious life

Religious life cannot survive in a community like this. Celibacy in particular is not viable except as a lived response to the Living God. Remove encounter with the living Person of God from religious life; remove communal, visible expression of such encounter from community interaction, and the religious community will soon appear in the true light of its inherent falsity. When a community stops actively seeking together the light of God on its life, that community has become either a fossil or just a group of individuals living together for some practical, intramundane purpose. It is not a religious community or a Christian community in the full and authentic sense of the terms.

I do not want to oversimplify. I know it is possible for a community to actively seek the will of God together without formal periods of communal reflection on the Scriptures. Such seeking goes on through all sorts of faith encounters between members of the community. These take place sometimes between two or three who are gathered together, sometimes on the level of the group as a whole. These encounters take place under various forms and are called by various names. Some really are the kind of encounter they profess to be; sometimes they are not. I would only insist on two points: the first is that if a community is *unable* or *unwilling* to reflect together, with openness, freedom, and spontaneity, on the word of God, that community has reason to ask whether it is, in fact, a Christian community. Not every community of religious is a Christian community.

The second point is simply a suggestion or a question: Might it be that in our day some periods of formal, communal reflection on the word of God together are, in fact, a matter of *necessity* and not just one optional means of forming Christian community? I would not presume to say definitively that this is so: the variety of persons and graces in the Church is too great to allow for an absolute statement of this kind. But unless a given community can identify what its positive experience is of actively seeking the direction of the Living God in its life in response to the word of Scripture, that community has reason to question its integrity as a Christian community.

It may be — who would presume to say? — that in other ages the will of God for religious seemed so simple, the direction they should follow so clear, that a community could have this sense of unity in response to God's direction just by following a pattern laid down since time immemorial by generations of religious and specified for a particular group by the words of the founder in the Rule. But in our day not one, but all religious communities have been instructed by the Church to return to the sources of Christian life and seek a renewal through prayer and daily reflection on the Scripture. We are to seek a renewal of spirit and a valid adaptation of our lives to the changed conditions of the times. Renewal must be grounded in the word of God, and especially on the following of Christ as proposed in the Gospel. It must be faithful to the authentic charism and spirit of the founder. And it must go forward under the influence of the Holy Spirit. This requires personal prayer and response under the guidance of the Church.[1]

Since it is the communities as such that are called upon to renew themselves, and not just individuals within the communities, it follows that all of this effort is to be a *communal* enterprise. Then it would seem that prayer and reflection on the Scriptures must in some way become communal also. All must seek together to discern the will of God for the community. No particular method imposes itself. But what will be normative for all methods is the *spirit* that we find shining forth through the accounts of communal decision-making that appear in the *Acts of the Apostles*. In the *Acts* sometimes the whole community meets; sometimes just the elders and leaders. Sometimes the decision seems to be made by one person (as when Peter announced that a successor to Judas must be chosen, and when he ordered that Cornelius and his fellow pagans should be baptized: *Acts* 1: 21 and 10: 48). Usually it is the "apostles and elders" who come to an agreement on what is to be done. But however the decision is made, it is always presented to the community for their confirmation and acceptance. And the grounds appealed to as a basis for discernment and acceptance are constant: the *word of God in Scripture* and the *experience of the Holy Spirit* acting in and through the members of the community. The apostles are challenged about

[1] *Vatican II,* "Decree on the Appropriate Renewal of Religious Life", paragraphs 2 and 6, (Abbott, pp. 468-71).

their decisions and are not threatened by this. They take the challenges for granted. Peter, when criticized for entering the houses of pagan and eating with them, describes how the Holy Spirit acted in him and in the pagans, and "this account satisfied them, and they gave glory to God." They experienced in this the continuing self-revelation of the Living God:" 'God,' they said, 'can evidently grant even the pagans the repentance that leads to life.' " (*Acts,* 11: 18). Thus they discovered something new about Him — and discovered it as a community. Paul and Barnabas, having been sent by the community on a missionary tour, found it normal on their return to "assemble the church and give an account of all that God had done with them" (*Acts* 13: 1-3; 14: 27). And in the decisive Council of Jerusalem, when it was decided by the apostles and elders not to burden pagan converts with observance of the Jewish Law, the basis for the decision was Scripture and the community's recognition of the action of the Holy Spirit. (*Acts* 15: 1-35).

What makes the community of the *Acts* appear as a Christian community is their constant referral of all that they were and all that they did to the reality of Jesus risen and acting in their midst. No decision was made except in the light of His word and the experience of His Spirit poured out on them as a result of His Resurrection. Praying spontaneously together, seeking His will together in prayer and reflection on the Scripture, discerning together in the light of each one's experience of the Holy Spirit, this was what it meant to be together as a Christian community. Not to do these things would have been as inconceivable to them as life without breathing.

In our own case, if the day should come when we find it impossible, or just not worth the effort to breathe together in this way, this might well be the sign that we have communally lost our will to live.

PART FOUR

CHARACTERISTICS OF RELIGIOUS LIFE

CHAPTER TEN

Religious Life and Celebration

We usually think of community prayer in terms
of petition or praise. We gather to ask the Lord's
help in our needs, or to proclaim His goodness through
the Psalms. But the deepest meaning of community
prayer considered, not as communal reflection on
the Scripture, but as *liturgy,* is *celebration.*

Liturgy and celebration are the same reality. We
can come together to reflect on God's word (and
this, of course, can also take place within liturgy),
or we can come together to celebrate the reality of
that word in our lives. It is the nature of this celebration and its particular place in religious life that
we wish to look at now.[1]

The need to celebrate

The need to celebrate is rooted in the basic insecurity all human beings feel when confronted with

[1] This and the next two chapters were inspired by a workshop on liturgy given to the community of Nazareth House of
the Lord in Memphis, Tennessee, by Father Patrick Regan,
O.S.B. of St. Joseph's Abbey, Covington, Louisiana. Father
Patrick deserves credit for the good, but not blame for the
bad in what follows.

changes we can do nothing about. Change alienates us from our environment. We had just got ourselves oriented, got "settled in", fixed our sense of direction, and established our relationships with all the things around us — and then the whole picture changes, leaving us in a sense "outside" of it. So we have to shift in our turn, reintegrate ourselves into the whole picture again, get settled in new relationships. Celebration is an act of conscious reintegration.

A child is born. Something new has entered our universe, something we must adjust ourselves to relate to. We celebrate his birth, proclaim his place in our lives, proclaim the relationships we accept with him. Then he is assimilated and life can go on again, its course slightly altered but established and stable again until the next event.

Or our birthday comes around. A milestone has been reached in our lives. We are no longer what we were, but a creature grown older — and grown different — by one year. We need to face that, to assume its meaning consciously into our lives, to reintegrate ourselves into the universe, accept life again on this new basis.

Celebration is in order whenever an event takes place that changes our lives. We call such occurrences "threshold events", liminal experiences. They can be *cosmic,* such as the daily thresholds of dawn and sunset, the mid-point threshold of noon, the monthly threshold of the new moon, the changing of the seasons or the years, the birth and dying of crops and plants, eclipses of the moon and the sun, the passage of storms and earthquakes. They can also be *historical* events: victories, defeats, anniversaries; or the free establishment of *new relationships* by commitment: marriage vows, feudal oaths, allegiance to new governments, civic and religious covenants.

Celebrations and perseverance in commitment

We should notice here that some celebrations help us readjust to happenings that take place outside of us, so to speak, and completely beyond our control. Other celebrations help us to re-affirm, re-commit ourselves to relationships we have freely accepted. Human beings are not angels: the angels, being pure spirits, act with their whole natures at once. When an angel says yes, it is yes with his whole being. There is nothing "left over" to serve as the starting point of a conversion, a change of heart. Angels are like kingdoms with no spatial extension: when they are occupied there is no corner left unoccupied that might provide a beachhead for invasion. That is why the angels won or lost salvation in one act: their first yes or no was final; it filled all their existential space. But human beings are not pure spirits; we act with one part of ourselves at a time. Our right hand might not know what our left hand is doing. Our minds might be bent on fasting while our stomachs are being invaded and occupied by hunger. Our wills rule over us like weak monarchs in a vast land; we make decisions and send out decrees that are largely ignored outside the capital city of our heads. On the level of our emotional lives and our physical lives, things go on with a momentum of their own, following their own laws. A change in our wills is often like a reversal of the engines in a landing jet: the motors are full-speed reverse, but the plane is still going forward by the inertia of its previous movement.

This means that any relationship we freely commit ourselves to as humans is going to be constantly threatened or called into question by change. We grow beyond our original understanding of the relationship, and feel the need to reaffirm it on the level of a deeper, an altered comprehension. Or the relationship gets beyond us, as it were, events and evolutions taking place faster than we can understand them or adjust to them. Neither we, nor the persons we relate to, nor the circumstances in which we relate to each other remain stable. That is why there is a constant, a re-occuring need for reaffirmation of the relationship, for re-integration of oneself into the relationship on a new level. All human relationships are subject to slippage. As long as the horse is moving we need to keep straightening ourselves in the saddle.

When there is a communal commitment, such as religious life — a relationship with God into which we have entered together with others in one community — then the reaffirmation of commitment must be communal and visible. I need to see that the others with whom I am bound up in my commitment are readjusting too, are reaffirming their commitment, that the whole community is being reintegrated into the new situation without losing its identity. I need confirmation, not only of my continuing relationship with God, but also of my continuing relationship with the other members of my community. We navigate as a fleet: when one ship points up to sail closer to the wind, all the ships must point up at the same time or the fleet will find itself on divergent courses, headed for disintegration.

Celebration and change

Every change is threatening to man, even joyful changes. This is because every change confronts man with his own changeableness, his own limitation, his own powerlessness. Man is as powerless to prevent his own death as he is to prevent the tide from going out or the leaves from falling. He is weakness and littleness in a universe that is beyond his control, enjoying for a moment the gift of life that likewise comes and goes by the power of a Source beyond his control.

Change confronts man with mystery — with all that
he does not know and all he could never know or
understand; with the limitation of his intellect, the
ignorance of his mind. Change speaks to man of uncertainty: the uncertainty of his truth, the uncertain
continuance of his present situation, of life itself:

> Margaret, are you grieving
> Over Goldengrove unleaving?
> Leaves like the things of man, you
> With your fresh thoughts care for, can you?
> Ah! as the heart grows older
> It will come to such sights colder
> By and by, nor spare a sigh
> Though worlds of wanwood leafmeal lie;
> And yet you will weep and know why.
> Now no matter, child, the name:
> Sorrow's springs are the same.
> Nor mouth had, no nor mind, expressed
> What heart heard of, ghost guessed:
> It is the blight man was born for,
> It is Margaret you mourn for.[2]

If we turn to the moral order, every sin, every
failure, every changing day, in fact, faces man with
the non-totality of his will, with his potential for infidelity. Every change inside of himself or outside of
himself that calls for a readjustment and reaffirmation of his commitment places man in a "crisis situation", a moment of choice that will at one and
the same time be a judgment he pronounces and a
judgment pronounced on him. All change and changeableness just reminds man of the sand his hopes are
built on so long as his own fidelity or the consistency
of other human beings are the foundations of his
security.

And so we need to celebrate — to proclaim and
be aware of — the existence of something outside of

---

[2] Gerard Manley HOPKINS, "Spring and Fall", from *Poems and Prose of Gerard Manley Hopkins*, ed., W. H. Gardner (Penguin Books, 1971), p. 50.

man that provides him with an element of certitude and stability for his life.

In the light of all this we can see the following values in community prayer as celebration.

Celebration facilitates our "passing over"

First of all, prayer as celebration *facilitates our passage* from one condition or situation to another. Every "liminal event", every moment of transition in our lives, involves three things: *separation* from what was before; *passage* through the threshold event itself; and *reintegration* into the new situation or state of things. This can be frightening. It is a passage from the known into the unknown. It requires us to make decisions, calls on us to adapt, to respond in new ways. We are not sure we will be equal to the challenge. When others are going through the passage with us it is easier. We come together to confront the moment of transition together. We draw courage from each other's determination and courage. We are shored up in our faith by the visible evidence of others' belief. In addition to this our celebrations usually include some communal remembering, some re-telling of the story of how others have gone through the same moment of passage before us. We recall that Abraham left everything in faith to follow God into the unknown — and was blessed for it. We remind ourselves that our fathers left Egypt to wander in the desert for forty years, but that they did enter into the promised land; that the apostles left everything to follow Christ, and received a hundredfold, even with their persecution, in this life and in the next. We look backwards to the lives of our founders, of their first companions, of the Saints — and we see that they went through what we are going through. It gives us courage to face the present and the future.

Celebration and meaning

Secondly, to celebrate transitional moments in our lives helps us to face and to understand the *significance, the meaning* of these moments. Celebration is a way of recognizing that we are, in fact, moving; that something is happening, that things are not standing still. And through celebration we remain conscious that things are moving with direction toward a goal. Celebration keeps us from being just caught up in events and determined by them, like chips swirled about in a whirlpool. Celebration is a moment of asking "Why?" instead of just "What?" and "How?"

In our work-oriented society we have particular need of celebration, because work can become a whirlpool — an ever-accelerating cycle that dizzies our sense of direction. Every celebration is a moment taken out of work, taken away from work, to become aware of and to interiorize its orientation and its meaning. Celebration is a way of integrating our work into the whole picture of our lives, a way of reducing it to something that serves the purpose of our lives. Celebration keeps work from becoming life itself for us. In celebration we step out of the whirlpool for a moment to regain our bearings, to recapture our sense of direction. Then if we re-enter the whirlpool, it is with the strength of a fresh orientation, to use its currents for our navigation, not to be swept helplessly along by them.

Of the very essence of celebration is *leisure*. And leisure is of profound significance for man. Leisure, rest, repose is the meaning of the word "sabbath". It was by insisting that man take out one day a week to just rest, to do nothing productive at all, that God taught man the true nature of human existence on this earth. Man differs from everything else in the universe in this, that the meaning of his existence is not exhausted through his relationship with other things on this earth. Man's whole *raison-d'être* is not found in his contribution to the smooth running of the cosmos. Man has an added dimension: his relationship with God. And to teach man this God commanded him one day a week to just let the world get along without him. God himself "rests" one day a week, to show that God's own nature is not just to be the Prime Mover of the universe. God does not exist for the sake of the world, to keep the world going around; God has existence, is Existence, on His own account. He has His own life apart from the world and He lives it. And man, made in the image of God, does not exist just for the sake of the world either, or for any work he can do in it. Man has existence for the sake of relating to God. And one day a week he must simply take time off, time away from his relationship with the world, in order to show — to express to himself in a real way — that the ultimate meaning of his existence is not the work he can do in this world.

The religious community that does not take time off to celebrate the meaning of its life together will soon lose all understanding of its life's true meaning. Then it will identify its life with its work. Work will be the whole reason for the community's existence. For a religious community this is the beginning of the end.

The same is true of the community which prays together, but makes a task even out of its prayer. The community that sees its liturgy or its communal prayer as just another obligation, something to be gotten through with dispatch, had might as well not pray together, since its prayer is not really praying. The community that rushes through its prayers has made of prayer itself a task, and loses sight of God in the very tangle of the words it stumbles through. This is not to celebrate the meaning of work, but to make work the meaning even of celebration!

Celebration and the givenness of existence

The work ethic is founded on the assumption of man's power. The world is seen as standing in need of change, and man sees himself as efficacious to change it. There is truth in this, of course; there is something thematically Christian about man's acceptance of responsibility for the world. But human responsibility for changing the world must always be balanced by a very respectful acknowledgement of the divine *givenness* of the world and of our own existence through which we hope to change it. The world is not truly known unless it is known as the constant creation of God. From this follows a reverence, and even awe, of the world as being "out there" constantly by the sustaining gesture of God's creative hand. The visible world begins at God's fingertips. It is the ictus in time and space of His creative wave. And man's own existence — the very life and power he intends to use for the betterment of the world —is itself no more substantial than the airflow of that same wave. And so a third value of celebration is to increase man's *awareness of the givenness of the world and of his own life;* to focus his attention beyond the immediacy of things' "being there" to the fragility and givenness of that fact; to let him see all things as gift, and find in them the Giver who makes them to be for man and communicates Himself to man in and through them all. Celebration makes us poor in spirit that we might be rich in awareness of God.

Celebration that makes man aware of the givenness of the world is a prayerform which fosters and sustains that finding of God in all things which is prayer carried out into action. Not to take time out to celebrate the givenness of the world is to be taken in by the world, to be swallowed up in the vortex of the world's need and lose oneself as man in the ultimate swirling vacuity of the cosmos. When man becomes merely the servant of the world then both the world and man lose their meaning. Thus, when work becomes so important that it leaves no time for celebration, the work has ceased to have any importance at all.

If man allows himself to take ultimate responsibility for this world he dooms both himself and the world to ultimate meaninglessness. Man as God is absurd and his work futile. Man as steward of God is endowed with transcendent value and his work with enduring significance.

If it is God who creates and sustains the world, and hands it over to man to be cared for in stewardship, then man's work is directed beyond the transitoriness and relativity of the world itself; man's work has consequences that are transcendent, enduring. Celebration gives man a chance to stand back and look at the world as givenness, as gift of God, and relate to it in the light of its origin and end. Then man can work on the relative and transitory reality of this world in the context of its absolute meaning and value. This is the virtue of wisdom.

Celebration and the ultimate ground of meaning

And this is the fourth value of celebration: *to ground* man's work, and his life — and all the events that mark that life as relative and transitory in man's passage through them — in something *absolute, enduring, and ultimate;* that is, in God. Celebration is the survival of meaning and purpose. A community celebrates the meaning of its life together in order to survive as a community. Once a religious community ceases to ground its being together in the reality of God, and God's call to them, the community is living on borrowed time. No religious community makes sense, really, as a social club, a mutual help society, or even as a service organization. Religious life is the embodiment, the visible extension in space and time, of a faith-response to the free invitation of the Living God, or it is a delusion. Other goals, secondary but immediate, may seem from day to day to have a more visibly determining effect on our lives than the personal reality of God as such. Our communities may seem to contract and spring forward in response to the immediate demands of work; to stretch out and relax just in satisfaction of an appetite for leisure and play together; to reshape themselves and accommodate in response to the surfacing needs of every member. The immediate, the momentary demand seems to determine so much of our lives that we have a correspondingly greater need for celebration, for something that makes visible the ultimate ground of our being together, the identifying end that determines the constant nature of our community.

When a religious community comes together to celebrate its meaning and nature as a community, the celebration should situate the community's existence within the broader picture of the history and life of the People of God. In celebration we tell the *story* of others who have been called as we are called (sacred history). We listen to the *interpretation* they (the prophets) gave, by divine inspiration, to the events of their lives. We relate the truths we live by to the truth of the Wisdom literature of the Scriptures, to the truth of the Gospels. We hear addressed to us the commentaries on Christian community that come through the epistles and *Acts* of the Apostles. In all of this we place our experience, the subjective experience of our community, within the objective context of the experience of the People of God. We ground ourselves in sacred history, in orthodoxy, in the solidity of the certain, the revealed action of God.

Forms of liturgical celebration

There is a special reason why liturgical celebration is so important to religious life. But first let us make clear what we mean by "liturgical celebration". Liturgical celebration is any form of prayer together that helps us to ground the transitoriness and relativity of our existence in the absolute of God; in the sacred story of His divine intervention in human history; in the revealed interpretation of the meaning of man's life and the nature of man's relationship with God. Liturgical celebration is prayer together that places our life and action under the light of God's word, situates our experiences and our work within the power of God's own action on earth. It is prayer that helps us see ourselves and our life together as a community in the light of faith and in the context of the life and action of the whole Mystical Body of Christ on earth. It is prayer that helps us to understand and pass through the liminal moments, the threshold events in our day-to-day existence together; that keeps our commitment to God and to each other strong, fresh, and evident. It is a moment taken away from, apart from, work; a moment of leisure to help us appreciate the givenness of existence, the immediacy of our relationship with God, the presence of God in all things.

It can be the Liturgy of the Hours. It can be other forms of worship service composed by the community, so long as what is celebrated in the service is the objective word and action of God addressed to our experience. What we celebrate liturgically is not our experiences together, but God's action as clarifying, interpreting, and validating our experience and our lives.

The Mass, of course, containing both the Liturgy of the Word and the Liturgy of the Eucharist, is the prototype and fullness of all Christian celebration. In the Mass we celebrate Christ's presence in His *Word,* through which He speaks to us today with a living voice; Christ's presence in His *Mystical Body* on earth, in our brothers and sisters through whom He speaks by the gifts of the Holy Spirit; and Christ's presence in the *Eucharist,* in His own Body and Blood, through which He makes present to us in every age and place the reality of His own historical life, His own real and unique presence affirming to us today the words and gestures of all His historical self-expression on earth.

But the Mass, to be authentically and fully itself, must really be celebration in all of these ways. The three presences of Christ — in His Word, in His Body by the Holy Spirit, and in the Eucharist — must be brought out and made visible, made matter of experience. The Book of His Word must be treated with an attention and reverence that express what His Word means to us, what we believe it to be. The gifts of the Holy Spirit must be allowed expression in the Mass; the congregation must not be a crowd of inert and silent spectators, but a community of believers expressing their faith to God and to one another in freedom, spontaneity, and joy. And the Eucharist must be the center of the Mass, the peak of God's presence towards which the Liturgy of the Word lifts up our hearts, and in which it culminates.

Liturgical celebration as we have described it is of special importance in religious life. The very nature of religious life is to be a lived, an embodied expression of man's *being called to transcend;* of man's being summoned to *pass beyond* this world, to stand in the presence of the holy. To live as a religious is to proclaim every moment of every day that *life itself* is a liminal event, a threshold reality. Religious life is a constant, conscious expression of the three moments of every liminal experience: *separation, passage,* and *reintegration.* But these moments are expressed and lived as the reality of life itself. Let us look at each of these in turn.

CHAPTER ELEVEN

Religious Life and Separation from the World

Religious life is a conscious, explicit, constant expression of *separation from this world*. Even visibly the tone, the style of religious life is different from the style and tone of secular Christian life in this world, and it is meant to be. It is part of the overall service of religious in the Church to bear public witness to man's call to the holy through a visible expression of "otherness" with regard to this world.

Separation and Christian holiness

Man's call to holiness is not just a call to ethical perfection, to a life of moral uprightness. A call to holiness is a call to be "other than" everything created because it is a call to identification with God *as Person,* who is "totally other" than all that He has made.[1]

Christian holiness is not a state of assimilation into God the Creator through deeper integration into the cosmos. Our liturgies are not celebrations of cosmic events such as new moons and changing

---

[1] Cf. Rudolf OTTO, *The Idea of the Holy,* (Oxford University Press, 1968).

seasons, as if through harmony with the universe we could perdure in harmony with God.

Nor is Christian prayer a technique of achieving "inner harmony" in order to be at one with ourselves, with our own interior forces, and so with God.

Christian holiness is the free gift of participation in the life of God as Person, in the reality of God's own personal life that He enjoyed before the world was made. Our God is a distinct Person, not identified with the cosmos, "totally other" than everything in the universe. And this God calls us to Himself, to share His Being with us in a free, spontaneous giving.

To share in the life of God Himself is necessarily, in some sense, to "pass beyond" the confining boundaries of created existence. To be a Christian is by definition to accept life on another plane than that of this world. It is to embrace death in advance as a passing beyond, a transcending of this world to live in the world of God's own Life. Christianity is, then, by its very nature, a radical "break" with the ordinary level of life in this world.

Until a man has understood Christianity as a call to "break" with this world deeply and radically, he cannot understand the Gospel. The Gospel demands that we die to this world in order to rise again and live in it in a completely different way. To be reborn in Christ is to give up human existence and accept it back again on totally different terms. After the "surpassing knowledge of Christ Jesus" nothing can ever be for us, or should ever be for us again, what it used to be.[2]

All Christians must express in their lives in some way this "break", this separation from the world. Not

---

[2] Cf. Karl RAHNER, S.J., "The Ignatian Mysticism of Joy in the World", *Theological Investigations III*, pp. 285-287.

to express it is not to be aware of it. And not to be aware of it is to ignore the true meaning of Christian holiness. To draw apart from the world in some way, to accept to be "other" than the world in assimilation to God, this is the awakening of a conscious call to Christian holiness. We are called apart from this world to be holy because God is holy, and God is not of this world. Only after some experience of such separation from the world (which need not be an experience of actually "leaving" the world in time and space, drawing apart from it physically) can a Christian "return" to the world and find there the self-expression of the God he has come to know as Person. Only then can a Christian give himself with full effectiveness to the world in service as an instrument of the God of grace.

Separation as a sign

The expression of man's separation, man's emancipation from this world can take many forms. The *sabbath* is a sign that expresses our call to the holy, because the sabbath is an act of separation from the world. The sabbath is an act of separation from *work* in order to just *be,* to enjoy human life in itself. Through the sabbath man takes cognizance of his life in its similarity to the life that God Himself lives apart from the world. (Cf. Ezechiel 31: 13). To celebrate the sabbath is to draw apart from the world in *time,* to leave this world alone one day out of seven.

To go into the desert, into a monastery, or even to go into a church for a few moments, is to draw apart from the world in *space.*

To adopt an alternate *lifestyle* — in the way that religious do, at least — is to draw apart from the world qualitatively. It is this last expression of

Christian separation from the world that we wish to discuss here.

One of the distinguishing characteristics of religious life is the deliberate "otherness" of its lifestyle. Religious, even though they may lead lives of intensely active service in this world, and even though their spirituality may be thoroughly incarnational, even Teilhardian, are called to live and to express in a visible way the deep reality of Christian separation from the world. They are *not* called, as secular Christians are, to "live in the ordinary circumstances of family and social life."[3] The otherness of their lifestyle is a characteristic of their call.

What are some of the things that are "different" about religious lifestyle? The basic difference lies in the vows themselves, of course. Religious live in deliberate poverty, in freely-chosen celibacy, in voluntary obedience. But there is more to it than this. It belongs to religious life to make a point of being "other" than the world in those concrete details that establish the "tone" of one's lifestyle. Dress, for example, has always been taken very seriously by religious as an important expression of one's break with the world, one's consecration to God, one's proclamation of man's call to the holy. Religious tend to address each other in a way other than that of the culture: as "Brother", "Sister", or "Father", for example. There are certain taboos in religious life that are hard to explain except as expressions of the otherness that belongs to religious consecration. The ban on smoking could be an example of this. Prescinding from the health problem, nothing is immoral about smoking. It may be an indulgence, but many other forms of legitimate self-influence are

[3] *Vatican II*, "Dogmatic Constitution on the Church," ch. 4, par. 31, Abbott, pp. 57-58.

acceptable in religious life. Why ban smoking? Why is it that a cigarette and a veil — or a Franciscan cowl — just don't seem to "go together"? It is important for us to realize that there are many nuances of expression in religious life that are there simply to be a reminding witness that Christians are called to be "other" than this world, that we were consecrated at Baptism to be holy — and wholly — in God. Religious give a particular expression to this baptismal consecration by further consecrating themselves to be a *visible expression,* a *prophetic sign* of the call to holiness that is part of human life in this world.

It is not that there is anything *unholy* about the things religious give up: about smoking, or drinking, or dancing, or dressing like a citizen of this world, for example. To see something unholy in these things would be fundamentalist Protestantism. But there is a connection between accepting the vocation to live a publicly consecrated life as a religious and taking a distance from these things in order to give expression to the reality of Christian separation from this world.

Complementarity, not contrariety

The human race has need of people whose lives are the visible embodiment of man's call to holiness. In the Catholic Church this need is supplied by the religious orders. In Protestantism this need gives birth to new churches, to "holiness" sects whose error lies in the fact that their proclamation of separateness from this world is made a moral precept of Christianity as such instead of being presented as a vocation to bear a particular witness within the Church. And so the holiness sects in Protestantism see their way as authentic Christianity in *contrast* to and in *condemnation* of the way of other believers. But the religious orders in Catholicism see their way of life as a particular vocation that is *complementary* to and *illuminative* of other authentically Christian ways of life within the Church.

To make a *moral* precept out of the proclamation of separateness from the world is to return to the essentially pagan concept of holiness as ethical perfection. It is to lose sight of the Christian meaning of holiness, which is to be drawn into identification with God who is "totally other". We do not withdraw from the world because the world is bad (ethical holiness) but because we are being drawn by God's gratuitous Self-communication into what is totally other.

This separateness does not express just a *preference* for what is "better" in a relative sense, as one created way of acting is "higher" than another. It expresses rather a *consecration* to what is better in an absolute sense. Christian holiness is better than *all* ethical behavior in this world, better in a "totally other" sense, better in the way that God, who made heaven and earth, is better than, infinitely beyond comparison with, all that He has made. It is no "better" in a moral sense; nor is it more Christian, not to drink than to drink, not to dance than to dance, not to smoke (danger to health excluded) than to smoke. It is certainly not morally better to dress in a way that expresses a deliberate, an explicit break with cultural style as such (if we prescind from all questions of modesty, that is). And therefore, to express separateness in these and other ways is not in any way to say, or even to suggest, that one is morally better or doing a "more perfect thing" than those who do not express separateness in such ways. To express separateness from the world is simply to *remind oneself,* and others, of the holiness we are all called to.

To have this ministry of expressing within the Church the call of all men to holiness is not to *be* more holy oneself. (It is true, of course, that to express a reality through one's lifestyle is to grow in realization and appreciation of that reality. Because of this, separation from the world can be a help to growth in certain areas of the graced life. One becomes what one expresses). A nun is not more holy because she does not drink, smoke, dance, or dress like others. She abstains from these things because she has been called within the Church to *express* in visible ways the call of all Christians to holiness; to be a *reminding witness* that the holiness to which we are called does not ultimately consist in using or in not using this world, however well one might do so, but in being drawn totally beyond this world into identification with the "totally other" God. Therefore the religious adopts a different, an "other" style of life, for the sake of the prophetic witness involved in living this otherness as such. Thus a religious who conducts himself like a man or woman of this world is not guilty of doing anything in itself less Christian; he is just guilty of not being a religious, of not living according to his own vocation in the Church. This is, of course, from an ecclesial standpoint, about the most unchristian thing one can do: to refuse to contribute one's own particular charism to the People of God.

The mistake of the holiness sects is to identify *being* separate with *being* holy, thus making separateness a moral obligation and holiness a state of moral perfection. The religious orders identify being separate with *experiencing a truth* and *bearing witness to it,* thus making separateness one particular *means* to holiness and a *service* to the People of God. Holiness is the call of all men to become "other than" this world through graced identification with God. But it is the grace of identification with *God* that makes man in reality "other than" this world, not the act or fact of keeping any created thing at a distance.

Confusion about separation and religious life

Catholics have tended to misunderstand this in the past, and consequently have looked upon religious as being "more holy" than seculars because they were more distant from this world. Religious fell into the same misunderstanding and made it a point of virtue, almost, not to have any contact at all with this world. In our day religious have reacted against this error, but with equal misunderstanding, by trying to remove all signs of separation from the world from their lifestyle. In doing this they thought to show that they understood the world and so make their witness more acceptable to lay people. As it turned out, they soon discovered that with a lifestyle all but indistinguishable from that of single lay persons living in community they had no witness of their own left to give. And so many communities took the next logical step and plunged into the witness and apostolate proper to secular, to lay Christians in the world.

It would seem that the guiding ascetical aim of many religious communities is to live the good Christian life in the world. There is a new and healthy emphasis on being deeply and authentically human. Poverty is conceived of in terms of "simplicity of life," which should be the standard of every Christian. The vow of obedience is presented both in theory and in practice as a commitment to "seek the will of God in community." Obviously every Christian community, from the family through the parish and diocese to the universal Church, is or should be committed to this. And celibacy, while it remains an irreducibly distinct characteristic of religious life, is not held up in its distinctness as spousal commitment to Christ, but offered rather as a way of being more available to others in universal love for mankind.

In lifestyle these communities aim at an external manner of living indistinguishable from that of good Christian laypersons in the world. Obviously no group of people who are unmarried, who live in community, and who own all things in common will be living exactly like laypersons; at least, not like the laypersons we are used to. But there is no reason why laypersons — while remaining laypersons — cannot live such a lifestyle. Many, in fact, are doing just that today. Many laypersons, both single and married, are living in community, sharing all of their goods in common, and subjecting themselves to the will of God for them as discerned in community. They are not religious, and have no desire or reason to become religious. In fact, many religious are finding their own lives renewed by the evangelical fervor, the prayerfulness and spirit of wholehearted dedication found in these communities.

When it comes to apostolate, many religious communities are embracing as their particular concern that task which in Vatican II is presented to the laity as "their own special obligation."[4] This is the task of restructuring the social order. Religious are undertaking the reform of social structures, dedicating themselves to the achievement of social justice in business and politics. Meanwhile it is in the lay Christian communities that people — both laypersons and religious — are finding the answer to their need

---

[4] "Decree on the Apostolate of the Laity," ch. 2, par. 7, (Abbott, p. 498) and "Pastoral Constitution on the Church in the Modern World," Part. I, ch. 4, par. 43, (Abbott, p. 244).

for prayer, for spiritual direction, and for communal support and expression of faith.[5]

Separation and the authenticity of Christian social action

The purpose of these paragraphs is not to criticize religious for engaging in the apostolate of reforming social structures. It is the *proper* task of the laity, but there is no reason why some religious should not spearhead the Church's new movement toward assuming real Christian responsibility for justice in the world. The purpose of what is written here is not to *take away* from religious, or from the Church, any apostolic contribution being made by religious to the restoration of all things in Christ. It is rather to urge religious to reconsider what is proper to their own state of life, and to go further: to *restore* to religious life and to the Church the authentic value of a distinct, alternate style of life within the People of God. Without the reminding witness of lives deliberately separated from this world all the efforts of the Christian people to restore the temporal order — that is, to provide an order of things that responds with justice and love to the needs of man in this world while he is still in it — run the risk of degenerating into a merely humanistic secularism.

---

[5] We are referring here primarily to the covenanted communites of the Charismatic Renewal. But it would be impossible to list and distinguish the variety of Christian communities springing up in the Church today. Some of these communities, while defining themselves as "lay" communities, might actually be religious orders without the name. Our purpose here is not to fit communities into categories, but rather to ask whether that particular charismatic reality known as "religious life" is being realized and given to the Church today in all of its authentic fullness. Those of us who are called to be religious have a particular gift to contribute to the life of the Church. Our first task is to *understand* and to *be,* authentically and integrally, all that we are called to be.

Father George Higgins, whose name is almost synonymous with Catholic social concern, bears eloquent testimony to this danger in an address on priestly work and prayer. Higgins quotes Professor Louis Dupré:

> A number of well-intentioned people nowadays believe that the sagging cause of religion can be lifted up only by giving social interpretations to religious messages. Faith has everything to lose and society nothing to gain by such a change. For I do not see how religious considerations can do anything to social planning but muddle the issue, *unless* they express a transcendent dimension beyond social issues.[6]

The words are those of Dupré, but the testimony is that of Higgins! A religion of merely social concerns falls, paradoxically, into the same error as the fundamentalist "holiness" sects; that is, it reduces man's call to the holy to a *moral* holiness. Where the fundamentalists make separation from the world a *moral precept* instead of a *sign* of man's call to identification with God, the social Christians make the achievement of moral justice on a societal level in this world the whole of religion. It is when the *achievement* of social justice as such becomes primary rather than the *witness* that is borne to God through it, that holiness is identified with morality and Christianity with social action. This is a religion of doing more than of being; of works more than of faith; of ethical behavior more than of identification with God. This, Higgins says, is to "moralize" the existence of the Church. When the Church becomes identified with supporting good family life, justice between employer and employee, etc., she is being identified with matters that simply are not the center of any authentic concept of religion. In support of this he cites Alan Watts:

[6] Louis DUPRÉ, *The Other Dimension: A Search for the Meaning of Religious Attitudes,* (Doubleday), p. 3-4.

The present low ebb of Church religion consists in the fact that rarely, even for Church people, does it give the soul any knowledge of union with the reality that underlies the universe. To put it in another way, modern Church religion is little concerned with giving any consciousness of union with God. It is not *mystical* religion, and for that reason it is not fully and essentially religion.[7]

And Higgins draws his conclusion:

I would be the first to argue that the social mission of the Church, properly understood, is of paramount importance and has never at any point in modern history really been taken seriously. And yet, the older I get — *post* but hopefully not *propter hoc* — the more I am convinced that what Hotchkins says on this matter in his workshop paper is the simple truth: "The Church cannot find a future simply in secular concerns, however pressing and urgent these may be, for the Church is meant to be a community of the transcendent."

The operative word in that sentence is the word "simply". Of course the Church must be concerned with secular affairs. If I thought otherwise, I might be tempted to curse the merciless fate that has consigned me to this kind of work for my entire priesthood. But the Church must not be concerned *simply* — much less simplistically — with secular affairs.[8]

Father James Schall, S.J., wrote in *Commonweal* that, according to Aristotle, if man is the highest being, then politics (whose aim is to give man the good life in this world) must be the highest and only science. Everything, in other words, must become political. We can argue conversely that whenever any society, *even a church or a religious order*, adopts a

[7] *Behold the Spirit: A Study in the Necessity of Mystical Religion.* (Pantheon), p. 5-7.

[8] George G. HIGGINS, "The Church: Insights and Priorities for the United States," an address delivered to the General Assembly Delegates of the Paulist Fathers in May, 1974. Mimeographed copies were issued by the Paulist Institute, ed. Robert Moran, C.S.P., Boston.

THE SPIRIT PRAYS

THE PRESENCE OF GOD

AS INDWELLING LOVE

WHEN WE
    DO NOT KNOW HOW
TO PRAY
          IN WORDS
    ANY MORE.

G.A. MALONEY

system of priorities that in effect makes politics its highest work, that society is implicitly affirming that man must be the highest being it recognizes. It is possible, in other words, for a religion or a religious order to become implicit atheism. The problem as Schall sees it

> is that of the relation between prayer and politics. This is the classical problem of the relation of action and contemplation as it exists in our world. My initial conclusions are these: modern social and political movements — be they anti-war, ecological, or Third World development — have so identified religion and spirituality with their this-worldly programs that they are in grave danger of losing their religious foundation and justification which is the transcendence and mystery of God.
>
> Therefore, the need and longing for the monastery in the modern world is a sign of a rejection of the greatest heresy Christian theory can conceive, namely, the direct identification of the divine purpose with the this-worldly affairs of men.[9]

One of the functions of religious orders in the Church is to bear witness constantly, and publicly, to the fact that Christianity is not simply a this-worldly religion, a social ethic that summons God to testify in behalf of reform programs in this world. The need for this witness from the religious orders is greater in the measure that Christianity takes seriously the this-worldly dimensions that are integral to the Gospel message. The Synod of Bishops (October 25, 1974) has recently gone on record to reaffirm the "intimate connection" between evangelization and the liberation of peoples. What this demands of us is efforts to form a Christian community "with a conscience shaped by the social teaching of the church and committed to the achievement of national and international social

---

[9] "The University, the Monastery, and the City," *Commonweal*, April 7, 1972, p. 107.

justice."[10] At the same time Pope Paul VI points out in his opening address to the Synod that "politics for itself," even though it is a Christian duty, will "not serve as means for the church's evangelizing action."[11] And in his closing address, while approving the emphasis on human liberation, he reemphasizes the warning that "the totality of salvation it not to be confused with one or other aspect of liberation, and the Good News must preserve all of its own originality: that of a God who saves us from sin and death and brings us to divine life. Hence, human advancement, social progress, etc., is not to be excessively emphasized on a temporal level to the detriment of the essential meaning which evangelization has for the church of Christ: the announcement of the Good News."[12]

The very essence of Christianity, as rooted in the Incarnation of the Son of God, is to be fully divine and fully human at the same time. And since it is very difficult to preserve this mystery of fullness in thought and action, we are constantly running to the rescue of one or the other element, while leaving its counterpart to drown. While we strain to pull the human dimension of the Church up to the surface of our attention, her divine dimension is slowly sinking back

[10] Synod of Bishops, 1974, (United States Catholic Conference, 1975), p. 18. The Synod of 1971 had said "action on behalf of justice and participation in the transformation of the world fully appear to us as a constitutive dimension of the preaching of the Gospel, or, in other words, of the Church's mission for the redemption of the human race and its liberation from every oppressive situation." ("Justice in the World," *Synod of Bishops,* 1971, United States Catholic Conference 1972, p. 34). The responsibility of the layperson for this aspect of the Church's mission is underlined in Chapter 2, pp. 42-43, of the same document. I also develop this in my forthcoming book on lay spirituality, *Is The Good News Really News,* St. Anthony Messenger Press, Cincinnati, Ohio.

[11] *Synod of Bishops, 1974,* p. 6.
[12] *Ibid.,* p. 12.

into oblivion. And vice-versa. The clue to illusion or insincerity in the Church is the couplet: "Not... but..." The password of authenticity is "Both... and..." Cultural Christians, whether conservative or liberal in their orientation, will say, "The Church should *not* be concerned with social justice (or with praying so much), *but* with preaching the Gospel (or with relieving the oppression of the poor). It makes little difference what you put after "not" and what you put after "but": once you use a formula that sustains one aspect of the Church to the detriment of another you have put yourself outside the bounds of Christianity. The only way to be Christian is to accept fully all the implications of the divinity, and all the implications of the humanity of Jesus Christ and of His Church, with all that this calls for in terms of Christian prayer and action in this world. The Church of God must provide bread for the hungry while bearing unambiguous witness to her belief that man cannot live by bread alone. The People of God must be the leaven in the mass, the salt of this earth, the light shining in the darkness of the present time, while retaining their identity as a separated people, a holy nation, a people set apart. Christians must be found, and find themselves recognizing each other, as having but one heart and one soul, in the desert and in the city, in the monastery and in the market place.

The complementarity of religious and secular lifestyles

This means that there is not only a place, but a need in Christianity for members of the Mystical Body of Christ who will "seek the kingdom of God by engaging in temporal affairs and by ordering them according to the plan of God." These are Christians who "live in the world, that is, in each and in all of the secular professions and occupations. They live in the ordinary circumstances of family and social life,

from which the very web of their existence is woven."
This is their "proper function": to "work for the
sanctification of the world from within, in the manner
of leaven ...involved in temporal affairs of every sort.
It is therefore their special task to illumine and or-
ganize these affairs in such a way that they may
always start out, develop, and persist according to
Christ's mind, to the praise of the Creator and the
Redeemer."[13] This is the vocation, the service, the
special role of the *laity* in the Church.

It is worth noting that, in distinguishing who the
"laity" are, the Council first acknowledges the level
of popular understanding among Catholics, which up
to now has defined the layperson as anyone with no
"special" vocation in the Church: the layperson is
anyone who is not a priest, or a religious. But immediately the Council goes beyond this popular mis-
conception of the lay vocation and sets forth the lay
state as something to be accepted and defined in
terms of what is properly and specifically its own.
What is "proper and special" to laymen in the
Church; what identifies the layman's special grace
and role within the People of God, is *secularity*. The
lay Christian is a person specifically called to bear
witness to Christ as a member of this earthly city, to
be the leaven mixed in with the dough, causing it to
rise toward Christ until all that is human is recast as
the Bread of Life. "A secular quality is proper and
special to laymen."[14]

At the same time there is a place, and a need,
for Christians whose lifestyle constitutes a public, reminding witness that "the People of God has no
lasting city here below, but looks forward to one which

---

[13] *Vatican II*, "Dogmatic Constitution on the Church,"
chapter 4, par. 31, (Abbott, p. 57-58).
[14] *Ibid.*, p. 57.

is to come." There is a need for witness borne to man's call to the holy, to the transcendent, to the mystical. Something must reveal — dramatically and un-ambiguously — the other-worldly dimension of the Church. This is the specific vocation of religious in the People of God. "The religious state reveals in a unique way that the Kingdom of God and its over-mastering necessities are superior to all earthly considerations."[15] There are other ways to bear wit-ness to this truth than by becoming a religious, of course. But the religious way is one special way, and it is a unique way, a way proper to vowed religious in the Church, and a significant service to the People of God.

Part of the service of religious in the People of God is to bear their witness through *separation from the world* accepted and understood as a constitutive element of lifestyle. While all Christians are called to separate themselves from "this world" taken in the Johannine sense of the world as the milieu of sin and opacity to the light of God, a "world corrupted by lust" (2 Peter 1: 4) and "polluted" (2 Peter 2: 20), a "generation which has gone astray" (Acts 2: 40), still this is not a separation chosen formally and explicitly for its own sake. Christians choose to follow Christ and recognize as a consequence that they are "strangers and in exile" in this world (1 Peter 2: 11; cf. 1: 1, 17). They are "transformed by the renewal of their mind" and by that very fact no longer find themselves in conformity with their culture (Romans 12: 2). But the separation of religious is not, as we explained above, a separation from the world as im-moral. The separation from the world proper to re-ligious life is a separation from the world *as such,* from the world even as *good,* for the sake of the pro-

---

[15] *Ibid.,* chapter 6, par. 44, p. 75.

phetic witness contained in the fact of the separateness itself. It is prophetic separation. Religious separation is chosen for the sake of what the separation in itself *expresses;* namely, man's call to holiness, to be "totally other" than the world in identification with the "totally other" God. It is formally chosen, not just accepted as the consequence of a decision to accept the teachings of the Master. And what is chosen is separateness as such, a separateness not required by the Gospel, separateness as a style of life embraced in prophetic witness.

Separation from the world is not *distance* from the world; it is simply a style of living that deliberately expresses otherness as a sign of man's call to the holy. But this lifestyle may be lived either in physical apartness, as in the desert or cloister, or in the middle of the city, in constant contact with every current of humanity. Separation from the world is a characteristic of religious life as such, whether we are speaking of "contemplative" or of "active" communities.

Separation from the world does not mean *inactivity* in this world. One might be called to the apparent inactivity of contemplative life, (which is, in fact, an intense activity *for* but not *in* the world); or one might be called to engage as a religious in very active works within the city of man while living a visibly separate lifestyle. The essential is that the lifestyle as such proclaim in visible ways, that are not just synonymous with the perfection of Christian morality, that to be a follower of Jesus is to be called to identification with the Holy who is totally other than and infinitely beyond this world. The deliberate "otherness" of the religious lifestyle is a constant reminder to the Church that the goal of religion is union with the transcendent God, not simply the reform of human structures or behavior here below.

If one of the qualities that is "proper and special" to laymen is their *secularity,* it follows that one of the qualities proper and special to religious is *separation* from the world. This separation, let us repeat, *must not* be understood to be in itself "more Christian" than the secularity of the layman. It is not a separation from what is immoral or unholy (all Christians must separate themselves from that) but separation from spontaneous acceptance of the good, created world as such *as a sign* that man is in the world now on different terms: that all of God's Self-giving and Self-communication through the gifts and goodness of nature has been superseded by His gratuitous Self-communication through grace. And the sign that religious give is the gratuitous, the un-required "otherness" of their way of life as such. All Christians give, or should give, some signs of the separateness that belongs to the reborn as "a chosen race, a royal priesthood, a holy nation, a people he claims for his own" (1 Peter 2: 9). But the sign that religious give is to adopt a whole style of life that is the opposite of what the Council describes as proper to laymen. Religious do not "live in the world, that is in each and all of the secular professions and occupations. They [do not] live in the ordinary circumstances of family and social life;" it is not from these that "the very web of their existence is woven." They live in a way visibly "other," that proclaims a separation from spontaneous acceptance of the created world as such.

Separation and liturgical prayer

In order to persevere authentically in this life-style, without veering either toward compromise with the secular or toward the narcissistic minutiae of a self-enclosed world of sterile symbolism, religious have a special need for liturgical celebration.

The liturgical celebration of religious must keep alive their awareness of being a part of the Church — both in the sense of *belonging* to a larger body, and in the sense of being *only a part* of that body. Through liturgy religious fit the expression of themselves into the larger expression of the Church as such; they subordinate their own, subjective self-expression to the objective self-expression of the whole People of God. Catholic liturgy — that is, the liturgy of the Church spread throughout the world — will not subordinate itself either to the fussiness or to the fanaticism of any group. The liturgy of the Church catholic is flexible but firm, allowing for spontaneity and every authentically religious cultural tone. But the liturgy — whether of the Eucharist or of the Hours — remains the liturgy of the Church, and those who celebrate it do so as members of the total Body of Christ. To participate in the liturgy is to be reminded that every way of work or witness in the Church is only a service, a complementary service, within the totality of the redemptive Body of Christ.

To celebrate the liturgy is also to recall that the first concern of man on earth is to express his knowledge and love of God in reverence and praise. Liturgy is by its very nature an act of separation from the world, a going beyond the visible immediacy of things to the source and sustainer of them all, to the Living Presence of God.

This is why liturgical celebration is so appropriate, not to say essential, to religious community life. It provides both support and perspective to their life of separation from this world.

CHAPTER TWELVE

Religious Life: Transcendence and Reintegration

When Vatican Council II teaches that "the religious state reveals in a unique way that the Kingdom of God and its overmastering necessities are superior to all earthly considerations"[1] the Council does not mean by this that religious life is the *only* way to bear this witness. It is obvious that martyrdom, for example, bears this witness in a preeminent way. And so does the daily martyrdom of an authentically Christian secular life, a life lived according to the highest principles of the Gospel "in the ordinary circumstances" of family, social, and business life, in a world which does not accept or tolerate those principles. The secular Christian bears witness to the Kingdom of God by investing in this world and then risking his investment confidently day after day by adhering to Christian principles regardless of the consequences.[2]

But religious life bears witness to the priority of the Kingdom of God in another way, a way the Council qualifies as "unique," a way distinctively and characteristically its own. What is this way?

[1] "Dogmatic Constitution on the Church," chapter 6, par. 44, (Abbott, p. 75).
[2] See *Supplementary Note 9*, "Secular life as a way of martyrdom," pp. 269-276.

Separation, renunciation, presence

It consists essentially in three things: *separation from the world* as a sign of man's call to holiness; *renunciation of the world* as a sign of man's call to go beyond all human values, rediscovering them in God; and *presence to the world* as a manifestation of transcendent values already possessed here below.[3] These three elements correspond to the elements constitutive of every "liminal event," every threshold experience that gives birth to religious celebration; namely, *separation, transition,* and *reintegration.* Religious life does not just *include,* as every Christian life must, certain explicit expressions of these three elements; religious life *is,* in its entirety as a way of life, an embodied expression of these three elements of all graced Christian living. And so religious life constantly presents life itself as a liminal event, a threshold experience which finds its real meaning only as entrance into the eternal Life of God.

We have already spent some time considering separation from the world as a characteristic and a

---

[3] On the characteristics of *separation from the world* and *renunciation of the world* see Vatican II, "Dogmatic Constitution on the Church," chapter 4, par. 31; chapter 5, par. 42; chapter 6, par. 46; "Decree on the Appropriate Renewal of Religious Life," paragraphs 5, 7, 11 (contrast with secular institutes), 17; "Pastoral Constitution on the Church in the Modern World," Part I, chapter 4, par. 38. See also Elio GAMBARI, S.M.M., *The Global Mystery of Religious Life,* (St. Paul Editions, 1973), pp. 11-102; 125-128. Separation and renunciation are distinct realities that "say" distinct things, but in their expression they often overlap.

On the characteristic of *presence to the world* (as a sign of the reintegration of all things in Christ that is awaited) see "Dogmatic Constitution on the Church," chapter 5, par. 42; chapter 6, paragraphs 44, 45, 46; "Decree on the Appropriate Renewal of Religious Life," paragraphs 6, 7, 12, 13, 14, 15, 25; "Pastoral Constitution on the Church in the Modern World," Part I, chapter 3, paragraphs 38, 39; Gambari, *op. cit.,* pp. 149-152.

service of religious life. In this chapter we will look at transcendence and reintegration together. The final reintegration of man-in-transition here below is heaven, of course. And so the only expression of re-integration possible in this life comes in the form of previews, as it were — and only analogous previews at that — of what man's final, heavenly condition will be. Just as marriage is an image of Christ's union with His Church, so the religious state provides a few analogous foreshadowings, rough likenesses as it were, of what man's life in heaven will resemble. But these hints of man's final reintegration in the life to come are so closely bound up with the expression of man's call to transcend, to pass beyond the immediacy of life here below, that they will be treated together with transcendence in this chapter.

To be a Christian is to understand oneself as continuously *passing beyond* this world. For the Christian, life is by its very nature a *passage.* "The People of God has no lasting city here below, but looks forward to one which is to come."[4] Religious life is a public proclamation, in the prophetic language of the way of life as such, of the Christian's transitional state.

At the same time religious life is a preview of the final reintegration of all things in Christ. In the words of the Council, religious life "more adequately manifests to all believers the presence of heavenly goods already possessed here below." It "witnesses to the fact of a new and eternal life acquired by the redemption of Christ" and "foretells the resurrected state and the glory of the heavenly kingdom."[5]

---

[4] *Vatican II,* "Dogmatic Constitution on the Church," chapter 6, par. 44, (Abbott, p. 75).
[5] *Ibid.*

Paschal renunciation

The heart and soul of renunciation in the religious life is to be a proclamation that *nothing has really been renounced*. The whole meaning of the vows is to express faith, through the renunciation of real human values (or of the means to these values) on one level, that these same values are actually possessed, here and now, on another level. The religious renounces marriage in order to realize and proclaim the reality of spousal relationship with Christ. The religious renounces material goods in order to experience and express the Christian faith that all things are given to us already in Jesus Christ; that man's real treasure is found and is his already in the Kingdom of God. The religious vows obedience as a declaration of faith that man's freedom and his fulfillment are brought to perfection together in serving Jesus Christ, who lives and reigns today in His Church.

Through renouncing certain basic values, or the means to them, on the immediate human level, the religious becomes a visible sign of these values already possessed on the level of grace. Thus through renunciation the religious becomes at one and the same time both a reminder to the human race that this world is passing away, and a promise to believers that all things are being restored and re-established in Christ. (Cf. Ephesians, chapter 1; Colossians, chapter 1).

Preview of life to come

Religious life "foretells the resurrected state and the glory of the heavenly kingdom." There are aspects of the religious life that preview, as it were, what man's life will be like in heaven.

Religious celibacy should be "an outstanding token of heavenly riches" and bear witness to that spousal union between Christ and His Church which is already an established fact, but which will "be fully manifested in the world to come."[6] Celibacy is a visible embodiment and manifestation of the love-relationship with Christ that is available to every Christian now as an experience of commitment and which will constitute for all of us in heaven the experience of consummation. In addition to this, celibacy is a preview in the communal dimension of the universal love and unity that will exist among all men and women in heaven, when there will be "no marrying or giving in marriage," no need to pair off and specialize in communicating with each other, but "all will be like the angels in heaven," able to communicate their whole selves totally to every other person at one and the same time (Mt. 22: 30). In heaven there will be total sharing and communication of gifts between the Father, the Son, and the Spirit, and all who are "sons in the Son," "brides in the Bride," members of the Body of Christ in heaven. In short, as St. Augustine explains it, "In heaven there will be but the one Christ, loving Himself."

Perfect sharing between all men is impossible on this earth because we exist in the flesh. Because our existence and operation are conditioned by matter, by the flesh, we must live in space and act in time. This means that we cannot simultaneously be with all men at the same time and communicate with all equally. As a result people specialize: they marry and concentrate on sharing themselves totally with one other person, a spouse.

[6] *Vatican II,* "Decree on the Appropriate Renewal of Religious Life," par. 12, (Abbott, p. 474).

Religious, through their vow of celibacy, proclaim that man's limitation by the flesh is not ultimate. In refusing to specialize in sharing themselves with one human person here on earth they remind mankind that the ultimate sharing of persons in heaven will be a total sharing of every human being with every other.

The celibate does specialize, of course, and in very concrete, physical ways, in establishing a spousal relationship with the person of Jesus Christ. We have explained this above (chapters five and six). He commits himself to specific, visible ways of working toward union of mind and will and heart with Christ, the way one works toward union with one's spouse.

But the commitment of spousal union with Christ is at the same time, and intrinsically, a commitment to universal love. The Christ to whom one commits oneself is the Redeeming Christ: to become one flesh with Him is to become flesh given for the life of the world.

In Christ God the Son became incarnate in order to share the truth of God's own interior life with man. And so whoever commits himself to the Incarnate Christ commits himself to sharing the truth of his own inner life with all who are able through such sharing to grow in their knowledge of God. In other words the celibate, although his intercourse with men might be limited by the commitments or restrictions of his state of life, is not legitimately able to refuse to share his mind and heart with another *just because* he would prefer to keep his inner life to himself. He may withdraw from the company of men into a hermitage or into some other form of solitude; he may keep silence habitually or set aside moments for prayer and reflection during which he is normally not available to others. But the celibate can never refuse to share himself with another who could profit from that sharing just because he would rather keep his heart to himself. The celibate is a given man, a given woman. He is given to all. And his giving includes the gift of the inner mystery of his being and life, just as God's own giving does. In this the celibate state foretells the state of the blessed in heaven, when all men will be totally given and open to one another, naked in mind and heart to all as Adam and Eve were before sin clothed them with disguises and reserves.

The difference between the virgin and the old maid (or bachelor) lies here. An old maid (in the pejorative sense: to be a single woman living in the world is not necessarily to be an old maid) is a person whose life is characterized by the refusal to give herself deeply, totally, passionately to anybody. A virgin consecrated by celibacy is a woman who is deeply, totally, passionately given to *everybody* through her identification with Jesus Christ. This is not some abstract, theoretical reality that only exists as the conclusion of a theological speculation. The celibate has a specific, concrete commitment to *not* being an old maid. It is contrary to the vow of celibacy — that is, to the commitment to universal love implicit in this vow — for a celibate to be a closed-up person. As a wife must be open to her husband (and vice-versa) the celibate must be open to Christ and to the Body of Christ.

The celibate is likewise committed, and for the same reason, to being *interested* in every person. He is not just his brother's keeper; he is his brother's friend. He can never say to another, "I'm just not interested in hearing about your troubles; I have troubles of my own." The celibate must have the concern of a spouse for the Body of Christ.

What we say here of the celibate is true, of course, for every Christian. But in the same way that celibacy is a public, explicit consecration to Christ, in that same way celibacy is a public, explicit consecration to universal love. And in this way celibacy likewise proclaims and previews, in a symbolic way, the state of universal love which will be the reality of heaven.

Religious community life should stand out, the Council tells us, as an example of the community that existed among the first Christians, when all were of "one heart and one mind, and found nourishment in the teaching of the Gospel and in the sacred liturgy." Such community life reveals the presence of God here below, and foretells the joy of the communion of Saints with one another and with God in heaven:

> For thanks to God's love poured into hearts by the Holy Spirit, a religious community is a true family gathered together in the Lord's name and rejoicing in His presence. For love is the fulfillment of the law and the bond of perfection; where it exists we know we have been taken from death to life. In fact, brotherly unity shows that Christ has come; from it results great apostolic influence.[7]

Religious poverty should be such that it leaves no doubt that the community and its members truly "have their treasures in heaven" which it will do only if the religious are "poor both in fact and in spirit," able to "brush aside all undue concern and entrust themselves to the providence of the heavenly Father."[8] Thus the poverty of religious, where real and authentically evangelical, is visible evidence of the reality and value of the "Pearl of great price" given and available to men. It is proof of the power of the Kingdom to satisfy our hearts. It is proof of the fatherly presence of God aware of all our needs and

---

7 *Ibid.*, par. 15, (Abbott, p. 477).
8 *Ibid.*, par. 13, (Abbott, p. 475).

hovering over us with constant providence, freeing men to seek first the Kingdom of God without fear for our lives in this world. It also foreshadows the society of the blessed in heaven where all will live by the Life of God and no one will need to worry or to hoard, and where all that is good will be shared in by all men alike.

Religious obedience is presented by the Council as a way to "follow the pattern of Jesus Christ, who came to do the Father's will, taking the nature of a slave..."[9] Jesus, through His humility and obedience, entered into His glory. Obedience is a visible participation in the *kenosis,* the self-emptying of Christ, which has become in Christian understanding the way to the fullness of promised Life.

> ...He emptied himself and took the form of a slave... and it was thus that he humbled himself, obediently accepting even death, death on a cross!
>
> Because of this God highly exalted him and bestowed on him the name above every other name... Jesus Christ is Lord! (Phil. 2: 7-11).

To be obedient is to bear witness to the fulfillment of everlasting life, the fullness that is man's in surrendering to the life of grace and accepting the fullness of God. The glory that is Christ's is available to us, because His self-emptying is available to us. We share already in the glorification and lordship of Jesus because we share already in His humiliation and obedience. In the Gospel of St. John, Christ's "hour" is the moment of His death and resurrection inseparably implied in one another. And so for us, to be identified with Christ's death during life is to be identified with His life-after-death. His life-after-death is something we possess and share in right now. Even as we go about dying in Him, we are risen in

---

[9] *Ibid.,* par. 14, (Abbott, p. 476).

Him. To visibly die to this world in Christ is to make visible to the world the resurrection that is already ours in Christ.

Religious obedience appears or can appear to be renunciation of human fulfillment, since it is in fact a renunciation of control over two of the most important means to this fulfillment. Through religious obedience we truly give up control over the choice of means both to our own self-development and to the contribution we will make to this world — for we submit both our lifestyle and our work to the government of others. This giving up of control over our own destiny so radically and so absolutely in two such important areas of personal life is a self-emptying that is utterly without justification if Jesus is not in fact the Lord of our lives, if it is not He who ultimately governs and controls us through superiors. And so the vow of obedience is a proclamation that Jesus is Lord, that He reigns over His faithful on earth today as truly as He will reign over all in heaven forever. It is a sign that proclaims the reality of Christ's triumph. Obedience to Christ in His Body the Church bears witness both to the resurrection and to the Lordship of Christ. The vow of obedience says to the world, "Jesus is seated at the right hand of the Father. He is reigning over our lives today." And if Jesus is risen and reigns, then we who follow the way of His cross will also rise and reign with Him.

Renunciation is the key

It should be obvious that the principal *way* religious life manifests "the presence of heavenly goods already possessed here below" is through the fact and significance of the *renunciation of the world* that is constitutive of religious vows. The Council leaves no doubt that the way of the religious vows is a way of "renouncing the world" and "all things for the sake of Christ."[10]

The vows of poverty, chastity, and obedience entail real renouncement of certain values that Christians must look upon with "high esteem." At the same time this renunciation "does not detract from a genuine development of the human person."[11] And the reason for this, as we have explained elsewhere, is that through the vows we renounce certain human values on one level only *to find them again immediately on another, a transcendent level.*[12] Thus, the renunciation of spousal love in marriage bears witness and gives an embodied realization to the relationship of spousal love with Christ that is inherent in our Baptism. The renunciation of material comforts, consolations, and security through poverty bears witness to the comfort, consolation, and security that is ours through possession of Jesus Christ, the Pearl of great price, who is our treasure forever. The renunciation of normal adult human autonomy through the vow of obedience bears witness to the active, working presence of Christ in our midst as Head of His Mystical Body on earth, and reveals the possibilities open to us for that Christian maturity which is realized in real relationships of surrender and availability to Him. At the same time the vow of obedience testifies to the guidance and power of God given to us and to all men through His Body on earth. By renouncing autonomy on the human level we become in a visible way co-workers with Christ in God, and sharers of His power.

---

[10] *Ibid.*, par. 5, (Abbott, p. 470).
[11] *Vatican II*, "Dogmatic Constitution on the Church," Chapter 6, par. 46, (Abbott, p. 77).
[12] See *Supplementary Note 8*, (pp. 264-269).

Renunciation must be real

But for religious vows to be a witness to anything, they must first be in actuality what they profess to be in theory; namely, real renunciation of what this world has to offer through the very basic values of marriage, material possessions, and personal autonomy. Renunciation is a stance taken toward the visible things of this world that reveals the invisible presence of God. By renunciation we leave a visibly empty space in our lives as a manifestation that the space is invisibly filled with God. It is not that God cannot occupy the same space as creatures. God is in all created things; all created reality exists in God and has existence only in the measure that it exists in Him. God can be found in all things, and gives Himself to us in all things. But it is a basic acquisition of Christian experience (as well as the explicit teaching of God's word) that the presence of God is most clearly *revealed* in the absence of created goodness or power. The power of God shines forth in the weakness of men. The light of Christ is most unambiguously recognized when it illuminates manifest human darkness. The overwhelming gratuitousness of God's love shows itself in contrast to the sinfulness and selfishness of man.

Powerlessness and trust

The truth that the glory of God was revealed in the *kenosis,* the self-emptying of Jesus Christ, is a foundation-stone of Christian wisdom and practice. The Beatitudes invite us to believe that God's power and goodness are best appreciated by those who are stripped, or have stripped themselves, of the power and goodness found in the things of this world. The next chapter of Matthew ends with a counterpart to the Beatitudes: those who withdraw their trust from the means of power of this world can place their trust in God: Look at the birds of the sky, the flowers of the field; stop worrying. Seek first the Kingdom of God and everything you need will be given you besides. Finally, those who give up power on this earth will be endowed with power from above. When Jesus selects from those who have accepted His word the ones He will send to preach it to others, He instructs them to go forth visibly stripped of all signs of reliance on the means and provisions of this world: without money or coins, suitcase, wallet, or purse; without a change of shirt or shoes on their feet; without contacts or a home they know will receive them. They are to be poor in fact and in spirit, powerless like sheep among wolves. They are not to depend on knowledge or learning, worrying ahead of time about what they are to say, but they are to depend on the Spirit to speak in them when the hour comes. They must be willing to appear as fools, and be ready to accept persecution and even death itself as the price of sharing their good news with men.

Power from on high

But those who go forth stripped of all reliance on the means and power of this world will go forth endowed with the power and authority of God. "He gave them authority to expel unclean spirits and to cure sickness and disease of every kind." (Mt. 10, 1). In the self-emptying of men the power of God will appear. It was through God's emptying himself of what He was by nature, through God the Son's not clinging to His divinity, that the divinity was able to become incarnate and shine forth in the humanity of Jesus Christ. And the same principle is true for us: it is through our not clinging to what is ours by nature that grace is able to become flesh and shine forth in our humanity.

Nature respected but not relied upon

This does not mean that we *deny* nature, as if through the suppression of nature (its only substratum!) grace might more abound. The renunciations accepted by the Church as constitutive of a way of life authentically expressive of the Beatitudes are the specific renunciations of vowed poverty, celibacy, and obedience.[13] We do not renounce the use of every human means — as the Christian Scientists renounce medicine, for example, or some fundamentalist sects renounce scientific study and human learning. We renounce *reliance* on all human means, and express this by stripping ourselves of that which makes us able to *appropriate* these means, to possess them and hold them in guaranteed reserve as something that is our very own. For example, religious renounce not only whatever wealth we had to start with, but also all financial security for all time. We give up whatever we had from this world and we commit ourselves to being — and to remaining — voluntarily poor. Put very simply, we join the ranks of those who do not own enough to live on. And then we rely on God to provide us with all that we need to live on. We do not refuse to use the means of this world; we just refuse to make sure we will always have them. We insist on insecurity. We refuse any provision from this world that would assure us of adequate income. We accept what God provides from day to day but refuse to make anything He provides today the source of our security for tomorrow.

[13] *Vatican II*, "Dogmatic Constitution on the Church," chapter 4, par. 31, (Abbott, p. 57).

Secular renunciation

To live in such a radical insecurity is not something required for the perfection of Christian living. The truth is, an every Christian knows it, that there is no way *not* to live in radical insecurity in this world. The lay, secular Christian who has invested in a house, has a bank account and an insurance policy, and feels fairly sure of an adequate income from his job, business, or profession knows, if he is reflecting on the Gospel, that he is in danger of losing all of these from one moment to the next if he truly lives by the truth and example of Jesus Christ in this world. Every faithful Christian in this world lives under constant promise of martyrdom, whether his martyrdom (his *witness,* which is the meaning of the word) is given through the laying down of his life, of his job, or of his acceptance in society; whether he is called into the amphitheatre to face the sacrifice in small things or in great things. The Christian who does not experience risk in living his faith knows quite simply that he is not living his faith. "If they persecuted me, they will persecute you." Persecution is not just a possibility for the Christian living in this world; it is a promise. The Christian who is not called upon recurringly to die interiorly to all he has, to renounce possessions, family, and friends from the heart as a condition for persevering in the way of Christ, is not experiencing the call of grace.

Renunciation and purification in faith, hope, love

The religious life, with the renunciation that is proper to religious by their vows of poverty, chastity, and obedience, is not *more* of a renunciation of this world than lay, secular Christian life. Every Christian at Baptism renounces this world radically and definitely, even if he is not conscious of it yet! As we become adult in the faith we realize more and more deeply, and accept more and more personally, the implications of our Baptismal dying to this world in order to rise in Christ. When we have really accepted death to this world, and accepted it totally, we are ready for heaven. And until we do accept it we are not ready for the life of God in heaven. If by the end of our lives we have still not accepted to die totally to this world, then in some way not revealed to us in its details we continue to be purified of our attachment to life on the natural level until we are totally purged of the old leaven. This process is what is popularly known as "Purgatory."

The martyrs are presumed to have no need of the "purgatorium" because they consciously, freely, and deliberately gave up their lives in this world out of faith. They underwent the test of faith and came through victorious by the power of the Spirit. And this test every man must face. The way normally to be expected is the way of martyrdom, the way of bearing *witness* to Christ in this world in spite of risk, hardship, opposition, and persecution, until we emerge victorious over temptation, sin, and every threat or enticement of this world. This victory is consummated in the act of finally relinquishing this world — totally and irrevocably — in a deliberate Christian acceptance of death. The moment of death is the great moment of Christian affirmation. Death is the ultimate act of renunciation. It is renunciation, "passage," and witness all in one. To say "yes" to death is to manifest real faith in the Life to which death is only a passage. That is why death is the supreme moment, and a very special moment, of Christian faith. To die in Christ is to persevere in faith "to the end." Meanwhile, to live by the Gospel during life is an "exercise in Christian death." Every act of Christian renunciation is a preview, a "test run" of the passage from life through death to Life. This is why it is an exercise, a realization, and strengthening of faith.[14]

For a secular Christian, to live by the Gospel in this world is a way of renouncing the world even while remaining in it. The lay Christian uses the world, enjoys it, and at the same time *risks* it every day through uncompromising Christian conduct as a proof that he has renounced it from the heart.

Religious renunciation

But another way of facing the test is the way of religious vows. Through the vows we renounce the world *actively, explicitly,* and *permanently* as a way of expressing, and experiencing, the power of the New Life that was given to us with the Spirit at Baptism.

The martyr bears witness actively, but the actual *renunciation* of the world — of possessions, family, of life itself — that comes to him is something he endures passively. These things are *taken* away from him by men because of his fidelity to Christ. He lets them be taken away rather than compromise his life and give diminished witness to the Gospel. The religious, on the other hand, renounces possessions, family, and his own life in this world *actively* by the vows. He strips himself ahead of time of these basic values and points of insertion into the life of this world. He takes the initiative in giving up from the beginning things that could be taken away from him through the opposition of men. And it is this act of deliberate renunciation as such which becomes the identifying characteristic of his witness to Christ.

Through the vows, renunciation of the world is *explicit.* The secular Christian who lives by the Gospel

---

[14] Cf. Karl RAHNER, "The Passion and Asceticism," *Theological Investigations III,* p. 73 ff.

in this world is living a constant, *implicit* renunciation of the world, because to live by the Gospel is to constantly risk everything one might acquire or enjoy in this world. But religious vows are a way of declaring explicitly that all earthly values have been rendered radically secondary through the coming into this world of the Pearl of Great Price. Man can sell all he has now and lose nothing, because the treasure of the Kingdom of God is his. To bear witness to this truth, the religious does explicitly just that. He gives up explicitly "home, brothers and sisters, father and mother, wife and children and property" for the sake of declaring that in Christ all that one appears to lose by this is discovered anew and repossessed on a higher level in the life of the Kingdom of God.

Finally, vowed renunciation is *permanent*, in the sense that this deliberate, explicit renunciation of the world is made a constitutive element of a stable way of life. The secular Christian, who follows the way of martyrdom, lives in an enduring state of risk. Interiorly his renunciation of the world must be constant in order for him to continue bearing witness to the Gospel in a hostile and threatening world. But the actual renunciations he is called on to make are — or might be, at least — events that come and go in his life. He always risks impoverishment, for example, but he may not have to live always in poverty. The religious, on the other hand, vows explicitly to live in poverty, in celibacy, and in obedience forever, as a deliberately-adopted way of life. Actual renunciation of the world is a permanent, explicit, visible aspect of his lifestyle as such.

Complementarity of religious and secular renunciation

Because renunciation of the world through religious vows is an explicit, deliberate way of life, it is a way of bearing witness to the Gospel that is distinct from, and complementary to, the way of martyrdom, the way of secular Christians in the world. As a way of life it is neither better nor worse, absolutely speaking, than the secular way. But since the religious and secular ways are complementary to one another, we can expect to find advantages and disadvantages in each way insofar as living and witnessing to Christianity are concerned. And it is precisely the advantage of each way of life that will be, from another point of view, its disadvantage. The advantage of secular Christianity is that it is world-affirming; the secular Christian does not separate himself from this world, does not formally renounce it during this life except insofar as it is bad. And it is precisely this affirmation of the world that is at the same time the disadvantage of Christian secularity, because it carries with it an ambiguity: the danger of making Christianity appear as just a this-worldly religion. And so secular Christianity has need of religious life to bear witness in an emphatic way, within the unity of the same Church, that Christianity is focussed beyond this world. The witness to transcendence that secular Christians bear by the daily risk of martyrdom, religious bear in a way that is in some respects more visible, more explicit, and more constant by formally renouncing the normal means to certain key values of life in this world through the vows of poverty, celibacy, and obedience.

The disadvantage of religious life is that, without the balancing witness of secular Christianity, it could appear to be world-denying. But the advantage, and the contribution of religious life is the unambiguous expression it gives to belief that this world has been transcended through the coming of Jesus Christ. It is not only that all things are passing away — a message that could be nothing but existentialist despair. It is rather that all things have been passed *beyond* and are being re-established in Christ. Christians, and the whole of creation, are in a state of *passage* that ends, not in an absurdity of death and disintegration, but in the transcendence and reintegration of all earthly values in Christ.

It is, then, through renunciation that religious give real witness, give what we have called "real-symbolic" expression, to the common Christian faith and hope in the final reintegration of all things in Christ. Through the visible, undeniable fact of renouncing certain key values of this world in its present state, religious testify to all men that the present state of the world is passing away, has been transcended already, in fact, in Christ.

Religious presence to the world

To bear this witness it is obvious that religious must be *present to the world*. This does not mean that religious must be seen in the marketplace, necessarily, or cry aloud in the streets. There are many ways of being present to the world. The monastery on the mountain top can be just as present to the Christian consciousness as the Paulist preaching in the streets or the Jesuit teaching in a university. Saint Francis preached by taking poverty to the marketplace; St. Anthony by sensitizing the whole Christian world to the voices that cry in the desert. The essential is not that one be spatially present where the action is in this world, but that one be in fact a part of the action.

This means that religious life must be relevant to the needs of the world in every given age and place. There is no Christian vocation, religious or otherwise, that is a self-enclosed entity, totally determined in itself independently of the rest of the Body of Christ.

The grace and charism of every member of the People of God — including each one's calling in the Church — is given for the upbuilding of the whole Body. This means that no religious — or layperson — can understand his own vocation unless he understands himself in relationship to the Church at this particular moment of the Church's existence. Not only must religious be present to the Church, therefore; the Church must also be very present to religious.

All of this clarifies the phrases "renunciation of the world" and "separation from the world" that are constitutive of the Church's formulation of her understanding of the charism of religious life. There is not and must not be any psychological separation from the world, understood in the sense that a religious would just "leave the world and forget about it all." There are certain facets of the world that may be and should be forgotten, most of them the product of un-asked-for cultural conditioning. But the world itself is God's world, the world of our brothers and sisters, the world that God the Son came into, the world that is the center focus of God's redeeming love. This world must be always with us, always in our hearts, because it is the preoccupying burden of Christ's own heart.

How the world should remain present to us, and we to the world, is a particular question for each religious community to answer according to its own charism. It cannot be gone into here. The only orientation we would give here is a word of caution: it would be a naive mistake for active religious to presume that the danger of irrelevance threatens only the more contemplative communities, or those most visibly separated from the world. In fact, it is often the most active, the most involved, the most secularized communities which are most unconscious of the needs of the Church, and most irrelevant to the world. The very momentum of the mainstream of secular life into which they have let themselves be caught up can diminish their perception of the cross-currents of prophetic input welling up from the Spirit of God in our midst. The mainstream of secular life is seldom on course. This does not mean, obviously, that the Church should go into a backwater and stay there. The world has need of the Church to keep the cultural evolution of humanity directed toward God. But the Church has need of the guidance of the Holy Spirit to keep herself on course. This means that true relevance to the world is essentially dependent on the gifts of the Holy Spirit, especially the gifts of wisdom, knowledge, understanding, and counsel. To be simply caught up in this world, knowledgeable about cultural movements and events (including the cultural theology of the day), and wise in the ways of the world is not to be wise in the Christian sense. It is to misunderstand the world, because it is to be lost *in* the events of the world and lost *to* the context in which those events are taking place: the context of the order of redemption in which alone the events of this world reveal their true significance and direction.

The Church, then, to be relevant to the world must navigate in the currents of this world but not by them. This means we have need of members standing on the prow, on the cutting edge of the Church's contact with the world, constantly telling us where we are. And we have need of members standing in the crow's nest, looking beyond the immediacy of the present situation. We have need of navigators whose main concern is gazing at the stars. We have need of a variety of gifts in the community, the "common unity" of the Church. And the members possessed of these various gifts must be in close communication with each other, understanding and respecting the particular contribution each is called to make.

The purpose — and prayer — of these pages is that through them religious may be helped to understand a little more clearly the nature of their own call to contribute to the People of God and to all of mankind through a life of renunciation, of separation from the world, and of presence to the world, according to the Spirit of God, in the unity of the Body of Christ. Grant this, Lord Jesus. And further it. Amen.

Supplementary Notes

1. *The popular and theological understanding of the word "laity"*: (See page 27 of text)

Our confusion when we use the word "layperson" arises from the popular understanding and usage of words like "layman" or "laity". The word "layperson" has come to mean for us one who is *neither* a cleric *nor* a religious. This puts it negatively and creates the impression that the layperson is a second-class Christian whose distinction consists in not having chosen to become a priest or a religious. The "lay" Christian tends to mean for us someone who does not have the gifts and graces that priests and religious have. Lay Christians are "ordinary"; priests and religious are something special. This is the popular error we must be on guard against.

In this book we are, as a general rule, going to use the word "layperson" in its popular and imprecise sense to refer to Christians who are neither priests nor religious. But we hope to purify this popular notion from its negative or derogatory connotations. We have begun by establishing the proper, the technically precise meaning of the word itself, which really designates anyone who is not a cleric. In precise language, lay Brothers and Sisters in religious life are "laypersons". But from now on we will not call religious laypersons. We will reserve that title for those Christians who, in contrast to religious, are called to live and exercise their faith as secular Christians in this world. In contrast to clerics, laypersons are non-ordained Christians who have a positive ministry in the Church distinct from that of priests and deacons, and proper to the laity as such.

As we will see, the layperson's secularity is a *positive* characteristic, which gives a basic identity and orientation both to his spirituality and to his apostolate. The term "layperson", then, will identify a Christian positively both in terms of work and in terms of way of life. "Cleric" will identify a Christian in terms of work, while saying nothing about way of life (since a cleric can be either a secular or a religious). "Religious" will identify a Christian's way of life, while saying nothing about work (since a religious might be ordained or not).

It is impossible to develop here in proper depth the full meaning of the lay state in the Church. Here are some leads for further study:

Vatican II presents the characteristic of "holiness" in the Church ("one, holy, catholic, and apostolic") in terms of the exercise of the threefold ministry to which every Christian is consecrated at Baptism; namely, to function in the role of Christ as *priest, prophet,* and *king* (in our case, as *stewards* of the Kingdom of God). Therefore, the meaning of laity must be studied in the light of this Baptismal consecration. See "Constitution on the Church", ch. 2, par. 10-12 (holiness as exercising priesthood and prophecy), pp. 26-30; ch. 4 (the stewardship of the laity), esp. par. 31, pp. 57-58. And see "Decree on the Apostolate of the Laity", ch. 1, par. 2, p. 491; ch. 3, par. 14, pp. 505-506.

Karl Rahner treats this theme in "Notes on the Lay Apostolate", *Theological Investigations II,* New York (Seabury Press) 1975, pp. 319-330; and in "The Layman and the Religious Life", in *Theology for Renewal,* New York (Sheed and Ward), 1964, pp. 176-

183 especially. He also develops it in "The Sacramental Basis for the Role of the Layman in the Church", in *Theological Investigations VIII,* New York, (Herder and Herder), 1971, pp. 51 ff. For Rahner, as for Vatican II, the starting point for all reflection on the meaning of laity is the situation of the layman as a Christian *in this world*:

> The mission of the baptized layman to share in the task of the Church does not begin and end with the observance of peaceful Sunday devotions. It does not consist in any primary sense in Corpus Christi processions with the notables of the parish or the political party or the good Catholics. It does not mean casting one's vote in favor of the Catholic interest, nor yet in patiently paying the Church's dues. Rather, it implies an awareness, so deep and so radical that it revolutionizes everything, of the fact that the baptized man is constantly confronted with the task of a Christian precisely in that environment in which he finds himself and in which his life is passed, that is to say in the wholly natural context of his calling, in his family, the circles in which he lives, his nation and state, his human and cultural milieu. And this task consists in establishing the dominion of God in truth, in selflessness and in love, and thereby making what is truly essential to the Church's nature present in the setting in which he is placed, from the position which only he can occupy, in which he cannot be replaced by any other, not even by the clergy, and where, nevertheless, the Church must be. (Ibid., p. 61-62).

2. *The apostolate of the hierarchy and the apostolate of the laity* (See page 29 of text)

A chapter, or book, could be written on the nature and distinction of these two apostolates. From the standpoint of our own interest in this book; namely, the nature of religious life, let us just point out that, in a general and normative way, religious life engages a person in the apostolate of the hierarchy. The reasons for this are:

a) Religious life is a public expression of the life of the Church, acknowledged by her as such through her official approbation of religious communities. The life of every individual accepted into a religious community becomes, then, by that very fact, part of the Church's publicly-acknowledged manifestation of her own life. By this very fact and because of it the Church has the right, and uses it, to claim jurisdiction over the life and work of members of religious communities, and to govern them with authority in both their lifestyle and their apostolate, insofar as these engage the Church's manifestation of herself. (Cf. Rahner, "The Layman and the Religious life", in *Theology for Renewal,* pp. 162-165).

b) As a general rule and normally, room allowed for exception, Christians do not enter religious communities in order to reshape secular society as such, nor would it be proper to do so, since this is the proper and special task of the lay Christian in the world (see "Constitution on the Church", ch. 4, par. 31; ch. 6, par. 46). Christians enter religious communities precisely to make the vowed life of celibacy, prayer, poverty and obedience the mainspring of their lives and the source of an activity that they will engage in as an explicit expression of the Church's saving mission on earth. If, standing on this ground, they then engage in professions that seem indistinguishable from the work of secular Christians, they do so normally only with the permission of ecclesiastical superiors, and in order to contribute through these professions to the hierarchically-governed apostolate of the Church as such.

Rahner goes so far as to apply this reasoning to secular institutes, precisely because they "have made the evangelical counsels the center of their lives":

Their combination of the evangelical counsels with a secular profession (the possibility of which is in no way disputed) is, seen from this point of view, not a primary thing in their lives, but a tactical method in the service of an apostolate which is, basically, part of the Church's hierarchical apostolate. It is this apostolate which is, for them (in contrast with the really lay life), the sole aim; for it, all means, so long as they are useful, possible and lawful — including, therefore, working in a secular profession — are to be used.

("The Layman and the Religious Life", in *Theology for Renewal*, p. 179.)

c) A third reason for expecting religious to be normally engaged in the apostolate of the hierarchy is that if religious vows are somehow seen to be a consecration to the apostolate of the laity, then the real layperson, who does not take vows of celibacy, poverty, and obedience, begins to appear as a second-class citizen in the Church and in his own apostolate! Again, it is Rahner who asks the question:

...To penetrate and inform the secular sphere with Christianity, in a way that the clergy itself cannot do with its hierarchical apostolate... this is precisely what the laity are there for, the real laity without any qualification of the word. Here, precisely, is their own most proper and primary task, which belongs to them at least as much as the fact that they do not live in the state of the evangelical counsels. For if they did not have this task, precisely as lay people, what task would they have that was truly and inalienably their own? If we could not point to any such task, then we should be turning the layman from a person holding a particular state in the Church (with a positive justification for his existence and a specific task of his own) into a person characterized solely by the fact that he is inferior to the "real" Christians, the people following the evangelical counsels. But if this is false, if the married laity are a state that is really meant to be there in the Church as such, and not mere second-class Christians, then it is not possible to deny that they have, in full and ideal measure, the task of the Christian penetration of the world; that it is they, in the first instance, who have to sanctify the secular professions and practice them as the representatives of Christianity, and not the members of the secular institutes (or of the religious orders), who have made the evangelical counsels the centre of their lives.

(Ibid., pp. 177-179).

The lay apostolate is activity that is Christian, but not ecclesial; the personal and private initiatives of individual Christians rather than the public self-expression of the Church as such. The lay apostle is "sent" on his mission in the world by the sacraments of Baptism and Confirmation, but he is not "sent" by the Church to any particular task by any further mandate or sacrament (except through the sacrament of marriage, if and when he does accept the Christian role of spouse and parent). As Rahner explains this:

> The lay Christian has his rightful, primary, and absolutely inalienable task in the field of strictly non-ecclesial but nevertheless essentially Christian activity. The apostolate which belongs primarily to the lay Christian is precisely that in which he exercises responsibility for the world in those areas in which, in the nature of the case, the hierarchically constituted Church cannot do so as part of her office...

> ...The patience of a mother, the bedside prayer of a child for his parents, the social understanding applied by an industrialist to his business, the decision of a statesman in the political life in which he participates in the spirit of the Gospel and by Christian moral teaching, are relevant to salvation; but they are not acts of the Church. They live by the life of the Church, but they are not the life of the Church herself. They are Christian, but not ecclesial.

> *(The Christian Commitment,* New York, Sheed and Ward, 1964, pp. 66, 42).

See further Rahner's "Notes on the Lay Apostolate," *Theological Investigations II,* pp. 330-352.

In Vatican II see "The Church Today", ch. 4, par. 43, pp. 242-245; "Decree on the Apostolate of the Laity", ch. 5, pp. 512-516; and "Constitution on the Church", ch. 4, par. 32-33, pp. 58-60.

3. *Spirituality of function and of lifeform*: (See page 30 of text)

Obviously one's spirituality is going to be influenced, and one's spiritual growth should be enhanced, by whatever apostolic work one engages in. It is perhaps significant, however, that in the Council documents *work* seems to be the starting point for the spirituality of the priest and of the secular layperson. while *way of life* is the starting point for the spirituality of religious. More fundamentally, however, the apostolic mission itself of the layperson is seen to spring out of his situation or way of life as a secular citizen of this world. All this observation does is re-emphasize the fact that the identity of the cleric is determined by his function or ministry in the Church, while that of the religious is basically determined by his form of life, and not by his ministry as such. The secular layperson, as we have seen, is positively identified both by his life situation and by his apostolic mission as consequent upon this. See "Constitution on the Church", ch. 3, par. 11, p. 29; ch. 5, par. 41, pp. 67-70; ch. 6, par. 43, pp. 73-74; "Decree on the Apostolate of the Laity", ch. 1, par. 4, p. 494; ch. 6, par. 28, pp. 516-517.

From this we conclude that the first essential element to be discerned and developed in a religious vocation is a call to the *way of life* as such, and not to any ministry or work as a primary factor, unless the ministry is such that it is seen to be intrinsically dependent on a life of celibacy, poverty, and obedience. The lay apostle and the priest can rely upon the work they are called upon to do as a primary incentive for spiritual growth. The religious cannot — unless, as we have said, his work is of a sort that can only be nourished by an authentic life of prayerful celibacy, poverty, and obedience. One need not in this present age, and therefore one should not, become a religious primarily for the sake of exercising the priesthood, of reforming social structures, or of conducting schools and hospitals. Of themselves these ministries do not require religious life. If one is called to the religious way of life as such, however, one can be called to these or to any other ministries compatible with that way of life. Then the call to ministry and the call to vows blend in such a way that the two callings constitute one indistinguishable vocation, rising from the same primordial and mysterious root that is one's graced experience of call. In such a vocation, however, the religious must not rely on his work as such but rather on his Rule to provide the load-carrying momentum of his spiritual growth. Without fidelity to the values and ideals as such of the way of life to which he has vowed himself he will be unable to respond authentically and grow fully through the challenges and opportunities that meet him in his work situation.

All of this is in harmony with the teaching of Vatican II that in active religious orders "the very nature of the religious life requires apostolic action and services, since a sacred ministry and a special work of charity have been consigned to them by the Church and must be discharged in her name. Hence the entire religious life of the members of these communities should be penetrated by an apostolic spirit, as their entire apostolic activity should be animated by a religious spirit." ("Decree on the Renewal of Religious Life", par. 18, p. 472).

There are works the Church consigns to religious *because* they are religious, and works that the Church would not — at least in the past, perhaps — officially "send" Christians to accomplish in her name unless they embraced the religious way of life. This does not mean that the work as such determined then or determines today the fundamental nature of the religious way of life as such, which these communities were asked to embrace and modify to suit their apostolic goals. Each community is a tailoring of the same basic fabric of religious life which the founders were moved by God to adopt and adapt for themselves. (On this see Karl Rahner, "The Ignatian Mysticism of Joy in the World", *Theological Investigations III*, pp. 289-293).

Our next chapter will take up explicitly the question of "active", "contemplative" and "mixed" orders in the Church, trying to clarify more precisely the relationship of work to way of life in these communities.

4. *The meaning of secularity*: (See page 30 of text)

In saying that the very web of the secular Christian's existence is woven from the ordinary circumstances of family and social life ("Constitution on the Church", ch. 4, par. 31, pp. 57-58) the Vatican II document is developing the thesis that introduces the passage just cited, and which underlies the Council's whole teaching about the laity; namely, "A secular quality is proper and special to laymen" — to laymen, that is, as distinguished from clerics and religious. What it means to be a "secular" is probed in more depth by Rahner:

> ...The layman is a Christian who remains in the world, not in the sense of the profane... but in the sense that the layman must have a specific task towards the world and in the world which determines his 'status' in the *Church* and not merely in civil life. Being a layman, seen from this point of view, does *not* mean being a Christian who does not really have much to say in the Church and who is merely a passive object of the pastoral endeavors made by the Church (= the clergy) for his salvation.

A layman is not one who *for such reasons* occupies himself with those worldly-profane matters lacking any religious relevance which would occupy him just the same even if he were not a Christian. Being a layman in the Church... means rather, having one's place in the Church as her member and exercising her functions wherever there is the *world*...

For the 'world' is not merely constituted by sinful and rebellious opposition to God, Christ, grace and the Church. The world is also God's creation, a reality which can be redeemed and must be sanctified...

In this world the layman has his determined place according to his historical situation, his people, family and calling, the individual possibilities furnished by his gifts and capabilities, etc.

And he has this, his place-in-the-world, basically *independently of* and prior to his Christianity. After all, he is born before he is re-born... The layman is originally in the world in virtue of the *pre*-Christian (but not 'godless') position of his existence; in *this* place, and not in any other, is he to be a Christian.

This he must be, not just 'in addition', but by christianizing his original pre-Christian situation, which is the very essence of lay-existence, in such a way that precisely where there is the world and not the Church, the Kingdom of God may begin to exist through him as a member of the Church...

...It is important to realize the fundamental point that the Christian *qua* layman is distinguished from the non-lay (i.e. the clergy and the Religious) not merely by the fact that he has an original place-in-the-world even *for* his Christian existence (which is true of every Christian), but that he also *retains* this place *as* a Christian and for Christian existence as such, and does not leave it even in the fulfillment of his existence (at least not by living a new kind of life which takes on the permanent form of a new 'state').

In other words, when we rightly say that 'the Christian layman remains in the world', this does not mean that the layman is a Christian and in addition also a man, a member of a family, the father of a family, a tailor, politician, art enthusiast, etc. Rather it means that his being-in-the-world which preceded his Christian being, remains and is not changed as a 'state" by the fact of his being a Christian; but it is now both the material for his very being as a Christian and the *limit* of this being, as far as his *exterior* life and the structure of his state are concerned.

As far as his state is concerned, if he goes beyond the limit set by his original situation-in-the-world, he ceases to be a layman.

What has just been said provides us also with the right meaning of the expression, frequently used nowadays, the layman's 'mission in the world'. Such expression must always be understood to refer to a twofold fact: the layman is placed in the world as a member of the Church at a determined point, given prior to his Christian being, *and* this is positively and negatively the place of his being as a *Christian* (i.e. it is a calling and the limit of his commission).

("Notes on the Lay Apostolate", *Theological Investigations II*, pp. 322-324, punctuation and paragraphing adapted).

For a wider treatment of the nature of secularity, see Rahner's "Theological Reflections on the Problem of Secularisation", in *Theological Investigations X*, pp. 318 ff. In laying bare the false principles of "integralism" (which we sometimes call "clericalism") Rahner also uncovers the foundations on which the need, and the understanding, of lay spirituality are built. Integralism he defines as "that attitude, whether at the theoretical or at the practical (though unreflecting) level, according to which human life can be unambiguously mapped out and manipulated in conformity with certain universal principles proclaimed by the Church and watched over by her in the manner in which they are developed and applied." (pg. 322). If there are areas of life in which the Church, as a Body, cannot pronounce a practical, moral judgment, and yet Christianity must address itself to every element of human life, then obviously there are judgments to be made, and decisions to be taken, which the individual Christian must take responsibility for, not as carrying out the policies of the hierarchy, but as exercising his own proper function in his role as a Christian member of secular society. It is here that the proper ground of lay spirituality and lay apostolate must be acknowledged. The layperson's right to speak as a Christian about the affairs of this world comes both from his baptismal consecration as a judge of this world (I Cor. 6: 2) and from the fact that he has been called to *remain* in this world as a layperson, and not add a further consecration through holy orders or religious vows that would in real sense take him out of the ordinary society of this world.

The mission of the layperson is not a sending *away* from where he is to another place, or to another kind of work. It is a sending that comes to him where he is, leaves him where he is, but consecrates him to be *in* that place and in that state of life the medium and instrument of Christ's action on the world. The priest and the religious are called by God and the Church *out* of the normal circumstances of their lives, into a new state of life, from which they may be sent by the hierarchy to perform this or that specific task in the name of the official Church, under the jurisdiction and control of the Church's hierarchical leaders. The layperson is sent without any alteration of his state in life or of his situation as regards work, family, or social life. He is sent by the Church, not in the sense that the hierarchy sends a member of the Church to a particular ministry in her name, but in the sense that membership in the Church as such is a sending to be the leaven in the mass, the light of the world, the salt of the earth, to work for the Kingdom of God. For the layperson, Baptism is the sacrament of his sending, reinforced by Confirmation.

This special place-in-the-world that the layman retains — his secularity — is his distinguishing characteristic in the Church. The layperson is precisely the Christian who is *sent to be where he is,* and not sent to some other situation or service by the mandate of the hierarchy. This special mission of the layperson never has been sufficiently understood in the Church, and is not yet today. One sign of the continuing depreciation of the laity is the assumption on the part of so many religious that they (the religious) have the burden of engaging in the work of social action, in reforming the structures of society along Christian lines. Since this work is precisely and specifically (although not exclusively) the work of the laity, there seems to be behind this attitude of religious the age-old assumption that religious life somehow makes one a "better" Christian than the laity. Religious still seem to feel that they are competent — and more competent than the laity — to do any work in the Church. And therefore, if the laity are not reforming social structures as they should, religious should step in and do it for them, or show them how. This is to misunderstand the whole nature of the lay vocation in the Church. The layperson is not called on to reform social structures because he cannot do anything else. He is not doing this work in the world just because he has not been called out of the world to serve as a priest or religious. No, the layperson is called to reform the structures of this world precisely because his place-in-the-world makes him the best-placed Christian to do this. His secularity is his vantage-point in the Church. For the priest or religious to take over the layperson's task without the advantaging position of the layperson's secularity is either deep presumption or shallow theology. Unless it is done by way of exception, with humility and a conscious sense of inadequacy, of being out of one's proper role, it amounts to an implicit affirmation that religious life, or the priest-hood, of itself makes one better able to play all the positions in the Church — in other words, that to be a religious or a priest is simply to be a "better" Christian than the laity.

Secularity is not some "lower level" of Christianity that religious are able to descend to at will, or as occasion demands. Secularity is the distinguishing characteristic of a specific and necessary state of life in the Church. Those who are not in that state — namely, priests and religious — do not have that characteristic, or have it only in a qualified sense. And the value of Christian secularity will never be appreciated as it should be until priests and religious realize that the secularity of the layperson qualifies him for service in the Church that the priest and religious are simply not able to provide, precisely because they are not, and cannot be, fully secular Christians.

5. *Religious life as a "break" with this world*: (See page 32 of text)

The inter-related but distinguishable concepts of "renunciation of the world" and "separation from the world" will be taken up specifically in chapters eleven and twelve of this book. We just want to give some preliminary support in this note to the thesis that both of these realities are inherent in the very notion of religious life. We will treat them together at this point as the "fugasecular" aspect of religious vows, that "break" with the world that is proper to religious consecration, in addition to and distinct from every Christian's break with the world through baptism.

Rahner argues that renunciation and separation from the world are inherent in the vows of celibacy, poverty, and obedience as such. He uses — and explains — the ancient term "flight from the world", *fuga seculi*, to describe the vocation of every Christian with these three vows, be he a member of a purely contemplative order, a monk, a member of an active religious order, or of a secular institute. In this sense he maintains that the spirituality of the most active orders, even Ignatian, Jesuit spirituality, is a continuation of the spirituality of the monks in the desert:

> We must take note of the fact that Ignatian piety is and intends to be primarily 'monastic' piety; 'monastic' not in a juridical sense, nor monastic in the external arrangement of the community life of his disciples, but 'monastic' in the theologico-metaphysical sense which constitutes the first and last meaning of this word. What we mean to say is that Ignatius in his life, in his piety, and in the spirit which he impresses upon his foundation is consciously and clearly taking over and continuing that ultimate direction of life by which the life of the Catholic Orders, the *'monazein'*, was created and kept alive. Proof of this is the simple fact that he and his disciples take the vows of poverty, chastity, and obedience. And with them they necessarily take over the attitude of the *monachos,* of one alone in God far from the world. Ignatius stands in the line of those men who existentially flee into the desert in a violent *fuga sœculi,* even though it may be the God-forsaken stony desert of a city, in order to seek God far from the world. It is nothing but superficiality if one allows the difference in external mode of life between Jesuit and monk to mask the deep and ultimate common character which dominates the ideal of every Catholic Order.

> ("The Ignatian Mysticism of Joy in the World", *Theological Investigations III,* p. 281).

This is the reason why no one in religious vows can really be "in and of this world" in the same sense — the same good, Christian sense — that a layperson can. Rahner maintains, therefore, that even "the members of secular institutes are in a theological sense not lay people in the world":

Let us put to ourselves, simply and straightforwardly, what it is that we are talking about: people who, definitively, spontaneously and of their own resolve, for a motive which is possible only from faith in the incomprehensible word of God, renounce marriage; choose to be "poor"; and renounce, through obedience, the free disposal of their own lives. We can make the concrete forms of this life according to the evangelical counsels as variable as we like; we can cut out as much as we like of what belongs to the ancient monastic tradition and not to the essence of such a life; but, if we keep our sense of plain reality and know what these things involve, in the concrete, in terms of living, then we shall not be able to avoid saying that these people are not people of this world, not "normal" lay people. To renounce marriage in principle is to have no home in this world. Such a person may then have, from God in the name of Christ and the Church, an extremely intensive mission to the world; to fulfill this mission he may immerse himself as deeply in the world as he possibly can; he may practise a secular profession (and do well in it, in the service of his supernatural mission); but he no longer belongs to the world as does the "normal" lay Christian.

("The Layman and the Religious Life", in *Theology for Renewal,* p. 172. See also the pages that follow this quote, and the footnote on pages 152-154).

In the note that follows this one we will show the contrast, and the complementarity, between the two basic stances that a Christian can take toward this world: that of the secular, and that of the religious, the "fugasecular" person. Then we will explain more deeply the underlying attitude and choice that determine the nature of these two options. At this moment we just want to emphasize that this break with the world is taken for granted in the Church's traditional and official understanding of the nature of religious life, and by theologians of Rahner's stature even to the present day. (See also Rahner's "Notes on the Lay Apostolate", in *Theological Investigations II,* pp. 321-323).

Vatican II uses the expression "withdrawal from the world" with reference to contemplative orders (Decree on the Renewal of Religious Life par. 7, p. 47), but in this case the term refers to the particular detail of physical separation, not to the general concept of "separation from the world" as a total lifestyle expressive of a basic Christian attitude. This general notion of separation from the world, which is common to all religious, appears in the Council documents in many forms: for example, as implied in "renouncing the world" and "all things for the sake of Christ" *(Ibid.,* par. 5, p. 470). It appears in the insistence that secular institutes — precisely as contrasted with religious — are "in the world" *(Ibid.,* par. 11, p. 473) in a way that other religious are not. Since, as we have seen, the members of secular institutes have also *renounced* the world by the same vows as religious, the Council is obviously assuming here that ordinary religious live in a way that expresses a *separation* from the world over and above the expression inherent in the vows themselves. This same assumption is made explicit in a document that is not the official expression of the Church, but which reflects her quasi-official attitude at the present moment; that is, in the rough draft of the proposed revision of the Code of Canon Law for Religious. (I am using the French translation of Father Germain Lesage, O.M.I., that was presented to the religious orders of Canada for inspection and reaction in 1974). In this proposed revision "religious institutes" are contrasted with "secular institutes" in terms of community life, separation from the world, and the wearing of a habit as a sign of consecration:

> The public witness to be given to Christ and to the Church by (religious) institutes includes a separation from the world appropriate to the character and purpose of each institute, as well as a habit prescribed by particular law as a sign of consecration of life. (Canon 94, par. 2).

> (Secular) institutes are not bound by the law of com-
> munal living, and their members, who on the level of
> temporal things keep to their own way of life according
> to the proper state of believers, are not required to wear
> any sign of their consecration. (Canon 125).

Even more emphatically, the Council's insistence
on the "secular quality... proper and special to laymen", as distinguished from religious ("Constitution
on the Church," ch. 4, par. 31, p. 57 and in many
places I have referred to in previous footnotes), reveals the Church's understanding of religious as
people who are "fugasecular", who have separated
themselves from this world. This is so true that the
Council feels obliged to defend religious against the
accusation that they have "become strangers to their
fellow men or useless citizens of this earthly city"
(Ibid., ch. 6, par. 46, p. 77).

Further developments and documentation for
these ideas can be found in Elio Gambari, S.M.M.,
The Global Mystery of Religious Life, Boston
(Daughters of St. Paul), 1973, chapter twelve, "The
State of Consecration", pp. 125-132.

6. *The root and complementarity of secular and
    fugasecular life* (See page 33 of text)

The division, or specialization, of Christian life
into secular and fugasecular lifestyles stems from the
twofold reality of Christian love. Christian love, like
God's love, must be both *cosmic* and *eschatological.*
That is, Christians must embrace, and express God's
love for man *in the world,* as enjoying his own created
reality and that of other creatures (cosmic love); and
God's love *drawing man beyond the world,* to
participate in and enjoy the life proper to God Himself (eschatological love). These two ways of loving
are not contrary, but complementary to one another.
However, the *expression* of these two loves may take

forms that are contrary to one another, involving as they do contrary ways of acting towards one and the same object. God expresses cosmic love by calling man out of nothingness through birth; He expresses eschatological love by calling man into the All of the Beatific Vision through death. Birth and death are complementary expressions of God's love; and yet, as human activities they are contrary to one another. The Incarnation and the Crucifixion were complementary expressions of God's redeeming love for man; yet, as movements toward and away from this world they are contrary to each other.

The Church — i.e., the People of God — must express the full, the integral reality of God's love, as both cosmic and eschatological. It is difficult, if not impossible, for one and the same person, at the same time and in the same way, to *express* in any emphatic or radical way both of these loves. Hence the need for different lifestyles: the secular lifestyle to express God's cosmic love; the fugasecular lifestyle to express God's eschatological or transcendent love.

It is a fact of human life, however (as we shall explain in chapter four), that the attitudes we *express* are the attitudes we *grow in.* Hence the Christian who chooses, and is called, to express God's cosmic love will grow in that love more than another Christian will who chooses, and is called, to express God's eschatological love. And vice versa. At least he will grow into a greater human appropriation of that love: in conscious understanding and appreciation; in thoughts, habits, etc. From another point of view, to grow "into God" in grace is to grow into the whole reality of God, in whom all things are simple and one. So no one is "worse off" or deprived for having grown more deeply into one or the other love on this earth, and for having grown less deeply, humanly speaking, into the other. But the love one chooses to grow into will become a determinant of one's human personality. As a distinct individual, specified equally by positive characteristics and by limitations, by what one is and by what one is not, each person will be shaped by what he chooses to express and not to express in his life. Thus one does not simply "live" a secular or fugasecular lifestyle, or "give expression" to certain attitudes and values in the Church. Rather, one *becomes* a secular or a fugasecular person, and the attitudes and values one expresses become the reality of one's personal soul. We say this bearing always in mind, of course, that within the unity of the Church every person is both secular and fugasecular, world-affirming and world-transcending, embracing the reality of the Incarnation and that of the Cross in a total way. But every person does not, and cannot, grow equally into a human assimilation during this life of all the reality, and all the distinct though united mysteries of the Christian faith. That is why Christians need one another, and need one another precisely as specializing in the assimilation and expression of different aspects of the faith, in order that the simple Truth of God may find the diversity it requires in order to appear as integrally expressed on the created plane of men.

The distinction, and complementarity of cosmic and eschatological (or transcendent) love are presented and explained by Father Karl Rahner in "Reflections on the Theology of Renunciation", *Theological Investigations III,* pp. 47 ff., and in "The Ignatian Mysticism of Joy in the World", ibid., pp. 277 ff., especially pp. 283-287.

Rahner discusses the meaning of "flight from the world" in these same two articles and, in the same volume of *Theological Investigations,* in "The Passion and Asceticism", pp. 58, ff. These articles present flight from the world as a new centering, a centripetal rather than a centrifugal force, on pages 50, 54; 77-79; 283-289.

The need for distinct lifestyles, secular and fugasecular, to give this complementary witness to eschatological and cosmic love is established throughout these three articles, and in all we have already referred to in previous footnotes concerning the spirituality and apostolate of the layman. See especially, however, *Theological Investigations III,* pages 48, 54-56, 80-81, 288-290.

The basic attitudes toward the world which give rise to, and in turn are fostered by, the choice of secular or fugasecular lifestyles are explained by Rahner in "The Layman and the Religious Life", *Theology for Renewal,* pp. 147 ff. Here the consequences for the apostolate are also traced back to this fundamental choice of lifestyle and to the attitude toward the world inherent in the choice of lifestyles. We cite from footnote 10, pp. 152-154:

> "The world" does not only have the two meanings of "the world created by God" and, on the other hand, the "evil" world...

> Even the world in the good sense, to which a human being and a Christian is allowed to belong, and to some extent always must belong (since for a Christian there is not and must not be any absolute, utter flight from the world) — even the world in this sense has a strange ambiguity and obscurity about it... Even the good that is immanent in it... still has a dubious quality about it; the doubt whether it is in fact laying itself open to grace from above or has in fact (perhaps only secretly) closed itself against it... Hence the world is ambiguous in itself for a start.

> And hence ultimately we have a twofold relationship to it, a twofold position in it and toward it...

> Our basic attitude (or perhaps we should say... its dominant accent, which is of course what takes con-

crete form in a state of life) can be that of a life which represents... the fact that this world (even in its goodness) is not the ultimately real and decisive thing, that it has to be constantly broken open to grace again because it keeps shutting itself against it. (This is the attitude we call fugasecular).

And again, one can (and still be a perfect Christian) lead a life which proclaims the fact that grace has indeed come down to us, that everything is now redeemed, that the other-worldliness of grace has become this-worldly... (This is the attitude we call secular).

Insofar as the first of these attitudes (fugasecular) is dominant — that of a permanent breaking-open and overcoming of this ambiguous world by setting up concrete signs of the truth that, in its present fashion, it is "passing away" (I Cor. 7: 31) — the person who adopts it as the groundplan of his life is, to that extent, no longer in and of this world; whereas he who adopts the second (secular attitude) is still in it and of it...

As we have already seen in many places, to be "in and of the world" as the terms are used here is the essence of Christian secularity, the foundation upon which lay spirituality and the lay apostolate are to be built.

The secular and the fugasecular options of a state of life are not higher and lower planes of Christian response. They are equal, and complementary, expressions of the one faith that is common to all believers, but which requires specialization and diversification in its expression in order to be integrally, faithfully, and emphatically proclaimed upon earth. That is why the laity and the religious need each other, and need that each be authentically what each is called to be.

7. *The diocesan priesthood: secular or religious?*
(See page 36 of text)

The diocesan priest, technically, is in secular life. He does not take vows of poverty, celibacy, and obedience. He does not live in a religious community subject to a religious Rule.

However, the actual status of the diocesan priest is in reality a mixture of secular and religious life, at least in the Latin rite.

First of all, the diocesan priest is bound to celibacy. This takes him out of the "ordinary circumstances of family and social life" essential to real secularity. Secondly, although the diocesan priest has no vow of poverty, he is a mendicant. His salary is not designed to provide him with an independent living. He is dependent on the rectory for board and room, the funds for which are supplied by the parish through offertory collections. The salary he is guaranteed by contract is not really a living wage but an allowance for personal expenses. It may be a lavish allowance in most cases, especially in affluent parishes where the board and lodging supplied from parish funds are super-generous, but it is still not a salary intended as a living wage. As a result the salary is, or has been traditionally supplemented by "stole fees", Mass stipends, and extra, personal donations from the faithful. (In some dioceses stole fees and Mass stipends are being abolished or discouraged). Through this arrangement the laity have been encouraged to expect priests as such — all priests — to be poor. Having become accustomed to "giving donations" for the support of the priest, they then resent it when he shows signs of living more affluently — or even as affluently — as they do. If each priest received a known salary, and nothing more, and had to live on it, much anti-clerical criticism (and rumor) would lose its platform. The diocesan priest would be a real secular, living in this world financially on the same terms as his flock.

Finally, the diocesan priest has no vow of obedience. But he has a promise to obey his bishop. His relationship to the bishop is basically one of feudal servitude. He is "bound to the land", meaning the territory of the diocese. He may not transfer from one diocese to another without being "released" by his bishop. There is a stigma attached to leaving one's diocese because of a disagreement with the bishop. This means that the diocesan priest, like the serf in the Middle Ages, is not free to simply contract for work as a priest anywhere in the world. He is bound to his diocese. The results of this are that the bishop has, in fact, an extraordinary power over the lives of his priests. Their whole future depends on his will, even on his whim. He may assign a man to the "Siberia" of the diocese for life if he so desires. All advancement depends on the favor of the bishop. This means that a bishop is in some ways a more absolute ruler than the superior of a religious community. He makes what rules he chooses to govern the lives of his priests. The limitations on his power are mostly those of practical politics, not constitutional limitations. Religious superiors are carefully limited by rule in the exercise of their government. They are replaced every three to six years. But bishops are forever, and there are not really adequate provisions in Canon Law to protect priests from arbitrary government by their bishops. Since Vatican II there has been a movement among priests — largely accepted and even encouraged by the bishops — to set up checks and balances against arbitrary government by the bishop. Dioceses now have personnel boards and grievance committees, priest councils and senates. In small and quiet ways one bishop after another is being asked by his priests to take steps equivalent to the signing of the Magna Carta. It is rare today that a bishop does, in fact, govern arbitrarily or assume exaggerated control over the lives of his clergy. But this is a change that is more *de facto* than *de jure*.

It is not the purpose of these observations to place any value judgment on the details of this particular situation. Celibacy and poverty may be appropriate for priests. Even feudalism is not in itself a bad system. The purpose of this commentary is simply to point out that secular priests are not really so authentically secular after all. They have accepted a life-situation quite similar to that of religious in celibacy, mendicancy, and in the degree of personal independence that they renounce. Whether it is good to be half-secular, half-religious, that is the real question. Or perhaps we should ask whether the diocesan priest has accepted the worst, the least developmental elements, of both lifestyles. He is financially dependent, but without the experience or witness of poverty. He is under the paternal authority of the bishop, but without the protections of constitutional government. He is committed to celibacy, but without community support for his life of prayer and growth in the Lord. In many ways he lives a lifestyle that proclaims him to be in "separation" from the world, but he has no clearly-defined lifestyle of his own to identify with.

This book deals with religious life, not with the problems of the diocesan priesthood. But we may do well to reflect on the situation of those whose lifestyle appears to be neither fully secular nor fully religious. The saintliness of so many diocesan priests is a proof that no one can blame his own mediocrity on conflicts with his community or on confusion about his lifestyle. But the problems of diocesan priests can also lead us to ask whether is it not better, as a general rule, to be fully one thing or the other.

8. *Renunciation as a concept* (See page 43 of text)

The word "renunciation" has a negative ring to it, and we do not like negativism in our spirituality today. It also has a note of hardness, and we don't like that either. Some of us have been wounded by a notion that somehow was communicated to us in the past, without anyone's intending to communicate it: the notion that "holiness is hardness". Words like "renunciation", "asceticism", "mortification", "sacrifice", etc., recall to our minds the days when all sorts of things we had forgotten the reason for were justified just on the grounds that they were difficult. They could be sacrifices offered to the Lord, therefore they should be offered: as if the very fact that something was displeasing to us made it automatically pleasing to God. This kind of attitude tended to put God — implicitly, at least — in a very bad light.

I think I would help matters if we were to specify that the kind of renunciation we are talking about in this book — the *only* kind we are talking about here — is a renunciation that can be described in two ways: first, it is renunciation whose essential value consists in its being a *symbolic gesture*. Secondly, it is *paschal renunciation*.

Renunciation as symbolic gesture is the same reality that Fr. Karl Rahner describes as "Christian asceticism". Rahner distinguishes four kinds of asceticism: moral, mystical, cultic, and Christian.[1]

Moral — or stoic — asceticism is basically just self-conquest. It is something common to Christians and pagans alike. It is the self-assertion of reason

---

[1] See "The Passion and Asceticism", *Theological Investigations III*, pp. 58-85; *Spiritual Exercises* (Herder, 1965) pp. 69-79; "On the Evangelical Counsels", *Theological Investigations VIII* (Herder, 1971), pp. 133-167; "Reflections on the Theology of Renunciation", *Theological Investigations III*, pp. 47-57.

and will over passions and emotions. It is self-discipline. What it aims at is the total dominance of the free self over anything that is unfree in man: his emotional reactions, his physical desires. It is the ascendancy of *ego* over the *id*. Moral asceticism has gone by many names, some of them Christian. It has been called the struggle of soul against body, of spirit against flesh, of grace against nature, of the "higher", the spiritual in man against all that is animal and "lower". Wherever credit for man's strength in the struggle is given to grace, we obviously have a concept that is more than pagan, that begins to include the truths of Christianity. It is not our purpose here to distinguish between what is good and bad, merely pagan or partially Christian in all of these concepts, or in the realities which they represent. What is proper to moral asceticism is the emphasis on man's effort to overcome whatever there is in himself which threatens his freedom (with more or less assistance from God in the form of light, strength, and attraction), and the restriction of man's goal in these efforts to the acquisition of "moral virtues"; i.e. to habits of good conduct which, in themselves, are proper to the nature of man. (The moral virtues — prudence, justice, temperance, fortitude and their ramifications — are distinguished from the *theological virtues*. The theological virtues are faith, hope, and charity, which are ways of acting beyond the nature of any created being, made possible to man only by the fact of his sharing, through incorporation into Christ, in the nature of God Himself. The theological virtues are not powers created and given to man, but rather the power that is man's through God's acting in him in a personal way and catching man up into His own activity in such a way that man shares in God's own, personal action of knowing and loving

Himself. This is a level of activity that man cannot achieve by any measure or manner of effort).

Moral asceticism is necessary. It is part of being an adult. And in the beginning of our spiritual lives — in what the writers call the "purgative way" and perhaps even into the "illuminative way" — our greatest emphasis seems to fall here. Young Christians, like young human beings of any condition, are often more animal than rational. At least there is much in our animality — our physical passions, our emotional reactions — that is not really guided by reason or governed by will. And so the first step in becoming a truly spiritual man, that is, one surrendered to God and to the inspirations of the Holy Spirit, is to become an adult, a person. We have to be in possession of our land before we can surrender it. And so man first wages war on himself, and then he surrenders to God. These are not really two distinct phases, as if man first attained the perfection of nature and then attained perfection in grace! Nature is working by grace, and grace is working according to nature from the beginning. But in the first stages of our growth toward union with God, the emphasis is on what man can do by his efforts, with help from God, to reestablish the proper chain of command within himself. Man strives to build a strong ego, to dominate from the heights of his freedom and personhood everything that is "below" the level of conscious, rational free choice, everything emotional, conditioned, or mechanical. At this point man is most conscious of the need to be *dominant;* his person is, as it were, "on top looking down" upon all that challenges his freedom, whether it be the inside world of his instincts, passions, and drives, or the outside world of threat or enticement. Later the direction of his gaze will change. He will be more and more conscious of being *surrendered;* he will be "on the bottom, looking up" to God, whose inspirations have become his law, whose love his motive force. Then he will be entering the "unitive way".[2]

While man is struggling to gain mastery over himself, even with the aid of grace, his asceticism is in appearance very much the same as that of the pagan stoics; their literature will prove helpful to him. That is why so many of the early Christian spiritual masters drew on the writings of the stoics to instruct and inspire their own disciples. And since so many of us were first introduced to words like "asceticism", "mortification", "renunciation" when we were beginners in the spiritual life, and have thought or read so little about them since, we tend to identify *all* asceticism or renunciation with what we experienced in our early, voluntaristic efforts to "become holy" or with what we heard or read about renunciation explained in stoic terms.

Stoic asceticism is not bad unless, like Pelagianism, it pretends that man can grow in grace by his own efforts. It is not bad, but we outgrow it. Not that we ever outgrow the need to assert control over the anarchy of our passions, but as it becomes less of a struggle, we make less of an issue of asceticism. Beginners need stoic asceticism the way they need counselling on the human, psychological level (whether this be therapy in the technical sense, or just good human advice). The need for counselling evolves into the need for spiritual direction, so that while one has to keep living by good psychological principles, the emphasis is more on the way God is leading man than on the way man should direct him-

---

[2] Part of this explanation is drawn from Fr. Adrian Van Kaam, given during a workshop on religious vows at Catholic University, Washington, D.C., during the school year of 1969-70.

self. In this same way the emphasis in asceticism becomes less and less stoic, although man still has to assert the primacy of intellect and will over emotions, and more and more an emphasis on responding to the inspirations of grace and giving these inspirations expression in and through nature. This, as we shall see, is the Christian asceticism of symbolic gesture.

A second kind of asceticism is what Rahner calls "mystical asceticism". This consists in repressing nature so that grace might more abound, as if there were some automatic connection between man's ascetical efforts and his mystical growth. This asceticism is based on the assumption that there is some spiritual law of inverse proportions that makes man draw closer to the divine in the measure that he draws farther away from the human. The attitude of mystical asceticism gives birth to the idea that man will become more spiritual in the measure he becomes less physical, that his soul will have more taste for the things of God in the measure that his body has less taste for the things of this earth.

There is some truth, of course, in this asceticism. On the practical level it works to some degree — not because our ascetical practices can really make us grow in grace, but because sometimes they remove obstacles in us that oppose God's gratuitous giving. The heresy, and it is one, behind this asceticism lies in the assumption that there is in the very nature of man some "divine element" that only needs to be "released" in order for man to soar to spiritual perfection and the experience of the divine. In its root this is pantheism.

But the fruits of this asceticism do not all spring from its proper root. Some of its fruits are quite good in themselves, some merely harmless. We see in our day people turning to various regimes and disciplines

— dietary, physical, mental — designed to set them on the path of tranquillity, of peace, or even of the divine. Such prescriptions as yoga, transcendental meditation, health food diets, and other ways of stilling portions of one's human nature in order to bring other areas into consciousness have their value, no doubt. There are depths in man that he habitually passes over unaware; and at the heart of man's being in grace is the Divine Indwelling. There is a divine in man; not an element of his nature, but the indwelling of a distinct, personal God. With this divinity man can enter into dialogue. He can still his body, emotions, or intellect in order to listen better. But when the divine communicates Himself to man, it is by free, personal act, an act of distinct choice on God's part, not dependent on man's asceticism, not limited to it, not evoked by it. The God Christians deal with is a Person, not a stratum of consciousness. And His dialogue with man will in the long run activate man's nature, not silence it. Hence the watchword for authentic Christian spirituality always has been, and always must be, "fully human, fully divine". And this is true in the total picture of man's life even though there are moments when God stills this or that faculty of man's nature in order to communicate Himself without interference. The mistake is to believe that man, by silencing nature from his side, can achieve through this very fact communication with the divine.

Then there is "cultic asceticism", or "ritual asceticism". This is an asceticism based on the very human assumption that, before man enters into the presence of the sacred he should separate himself from the profane. Man should fast before prayer, abstain from sexual intercourse before offering sacrifice. Things good in themselves are considered not good enough not to contaminate an encounter with the deity. Prior to the Incarnation this asceticism was probably built on a foundation of fundamental spiritual mistrust toward the things of this world, especially material things, pleasurable things, or anything that has to do with the body. So much of man's experience of the physical and the pleasurable has been an experience of temptation or sin that he automatically tends to associate these things with ungodliness, as if sin came from these things in themselves, and not from his own heart. By taking flesh, flesh born of woman, God made it blasphemy to call anything human evil in itself. Jesus taught that nothing from outside a man can defile him; only what rises impurely from man's own heart. But still man's experience of what stirs up the selfishness of his heart causes him to keep looking on some things as "less good", and to presume that man is more holy and pleasing to God when he abstains from these things. Many Catholics today are against allowing married men to be ordained because they feel that the man who approaches a woman's bed, even in the holy sacrament of matrimony should not after that approach the altar of God. Food and drink should not interest the true man of God, and so forth. These are understandable errors, and there are threads of psychological truth woven into them. But they are not the proper truth of Christian asceticism.

Before explaining Christian asceticism properly so-called, we should interject a word about a kind of asceticism which does not really fit into any of the above categories, but which is still something quite distinct from what we want to present as the Christian asceticism of symbolic gesture. This is what we might call self-sacrificing asceticism. This is the asceticism which consists in giving up something we like or would enjoy, because by doing so we will be able to give more to someone we love, or do something for him that will please him. This is the asceticism of the man who, wishing to serve God as a priest and seeing no value in celibacy in itself, yet accepts to be celibate for the sake of the work to be done for the Kingdom of God. Or the asceticism of the person who fasts from meat three times a week, not for the sake of fasting, but in order to reduce meat-consumption in his country and leave more grain for the starving peoples of Africa and Asia. We did not include this category when we divided asceticism into moral, mystical, cultic, and Christian because self-sacrificing asceticism is not, strictly speaking, an asceticism. The sacrifices one makes here are not inspired by any ascetical philosophy or goals as such. What I have called sacrificial asceticism is really just love choosing to please another rather than please oneself. Faced with a set of alternatives, one offering pleasure to oneself at the expense of someone loved; and the other offering pleasure to someone loved at perhaps even considerable expense to oneself — one chooses to be unselfish. If we had to fit this into one of the categories of asceticism, we would call it moral asceticism, because it consists in doing violence to oneself for the sake of some concrete value perceived to be a greater good.

Finally, there is *Christian asceticism*. This is the asceticism of symbolic gesture, and its value is self-expression, understanding the "self" who is expressed to be man's graced self, God and man acting together.

Christian asceticism properly so-called is an asceticism which aims, not at the acquisition of moral virtues by one's own efforts; not at releasing some sort of divine or spiritual element in man by practising techniques; not at purifying oneself from the contamination of created reality in order to enter into the presence of the holy; and not even at proving one's love for God by setting His interests ahead of one's own. Christian asceticism aims only at giving expression to the grace that is within us — and this in real-symbolic gestures[3] that can have no other purpose or meaning except the *expression and experience as such* of Christian faith, hope, and love. Christian asceticism does not aim at any practical result, as moral or sacrificial asceticism does — unless it be at that most practical result of all, which is the creation of oneself as a person by self-expression in response to the grace of God. As we have explained elsewhere, (page 43 ff. of chapter four) this creation of one's person in grace is a matter of increasing awareness of the mystery of one's union with God, accomplished through the expression of His grace in our nature in radical, unambiguous ways.

The symbolic gestures of Christian asceticism are nothing but radical, unambiguous expressions of Christian faith, hope, and love, which is the life of grace finding expression in our lives.

What Christian asceticism aims at is not some practical virtue or result, but just the *expression* of the fact that the God of Christian revelation is real in our lives — that He is all the Gospel says He is, that He is "our enough".

To really say what God is to us, Christian asceticism must not simply proclaim that He is *preferable* to this or that value, to this or that other good thing. To speak of God in terms of comparison with any created thing is implicitly to deny that He is God. We do not choose between Tom, Dick, Harry, this house, this employment, this pleasure, and God. God is not on a level with created objects of choice: they are goods, while He is the unique Good; they are

[3] The expression "real-symbolic gesture" is explained in ch. 4, pp. 48-49.

means to happiness or a full life, while He *is* our happiness, our Life. They are something, but He is our All. What Christian asceticism proclaims is that "God is our enough". He is the Pearl of Great Price, containing in Himself the value of all other pearls. He is the treasure hidden in a field, worth a thousand times more than everything we can sell in order to buy that field and possess it. If we possess Him, nothing else that we can have or lose will add to or take from our existence.

This is why Rahner teaches that the goods renounced in Christian asceticism properly so-called are not just useful things *(bona utilia)* but also things so necessary for our very development as persons *(bona honesta)* that nothing in this world would justify the renouncing of them. Rahner includes under such values those very goods which are renounced by the religious vows of celibacy, poverty, and obedience; namely, marriage, ownership, and independence. (He includes the renunciation of material things here because he sees ownership as supplying the material prerequisites for the full exercise of freedom in the autonomous direction of one's existence).[4]

The value of such renunciation lies precisely in the fact that nothing could justify it except the new destiny offered to man in Jesus Christ. Hence it is an unambiguous expression — and experience — of belief and hope in that destiny. For the Christian, fulfillment does not consist in man's achieving his *end* — that is, in his operating in a human manner, having his full human equipment and using it well (a "sound mind in a sound body" or "exercising his highest faculty on its highest object" on this earth)

---

[4] "Reflections on the Theology of Renunciation", *Theological Investigations III*, p. 50; and *Spiritual Exercises*, p. 71.

— but in man's attaining his *destiny*: the possession of God through grace in this life and through the Beatific Vision in the next. The *end* of any nature is always a general way of operating, and a nature is determined, recognized, and defined precisely in terms of whatever operations it is structured to perform. When we recognize in a being an ordering of its structure toward an overall way of operating that explains the presence in the being of all its parts and determining characteristics, we then have a way of understanding the being as unified, as *one*. To grasp in this way the unifying principle of a whole complex of different sense impressions presented to us by a given object is to recognize the intelligibility, the *truth* of the object. The object becomes intelligible as a unit, as one, through a recognized ordering of all its parts and aspects to one end. This intrinsic, structural organization of the object to operate in a way that justifies its existence as a whole is what we call its *nature,* and it is this which makes the object intelligible as a being, as something whose existence as a single whole is intelligible to man.

But to recognize the end and nature of a being is not to know anything about its actual *destiny,* or even to know if it has a destiny. Every being has an end, which is a general *way* of operating. But a being has a destiny only if the one who brought it into existence happens to have made it and intended it to operate on some *particular object*. A chair, for example, is made for the purpose of holding up a human being in a sitting position; that is its end, and the chair is equally ordered to performing this function for any human being. But if, as a matter of fact, a particular chair happens to have been made precisely and solely to serve as the coronation chair of Queen Elizabeth II, that one moment of holding up that one particular person is its destiny. We can figure out a being's end; it is written into its structure. But there is no way we can know a being's destiny, or even if it has a destiny in any one particular object, unless the one who made it tells us his intentions.[5]

Until God revealed in Jesus Christ that He has made Himself our destiny — the one Object in which all the Truth, Goodness, Beauty and Being our minds can know or our hearts desire is offered to us to be possessed in one act — man was obliged to seek his fulfillment just by operating on this earth as best he could, according to the potential of his human equipment. In this context human life would be man's end and also his highest value, so far as his own fulfillment would be concerned. To lose one's life — even out of loyalty to God and His law, and even if the sacrifice of one's life were the only honorable, the only moral option open to one — would always be an undesirable thing for man. Man might have to give up his life as the lesser of two evils; given the choice, for example, between death or dishonor. But in such a case he would not formally choose death as such; he would *choose* to avoid dishonor at all costs, even if losing life itself were the price. But death could not be accepted as a good thing in itself.

Likewise, during life man could not formally choose to renounce anything constitutive of the fullness of human life on this earth. He might make the *sacrifice* of a personal good for the sake of some greater good to others, or because some moral

[5] For the philosophical background to this, cf. David KNIGHT, S.J., "Suarez's Approach to Substantial Form", *The Modern Schoolman,* March, 1962, pp. 219-239. A theological development in the light of the problem of nature and grace as handled by Fathers Henri DE LUBAC, S.J., and Karl RAHNER, S.J., can be found in my unpublished dissertation, accepted for the licentiate in theology by the *Séminaire des Missions* (Fourvière), Lyon, France, 1962.

obligation required it. But in this case he would not choose renunciation as such; he would choose the greater good and accept the loss to himself of whatever he renounced. A man might join the Foreign Legion for the sake of the "glory of France", knowing that he would have to forego marriage in a desert career. This would not be celibacy, or renouncing marriage as such; it would be sacrificing himself for his country and accepting the loss of marital fulfillment as a consequence.

But Christian renunciation is precisely the proclamation that, by renouncing personal values that reach to the very roots of man's way of being on this earth — values such as ownership, marriage, and independence, that radically condition man's stance toward things, people, work, and his own self-development in this world — man doesn't lose anything in fact. Christian renunciation proclaims that man's end has been superseded by his destiny; that even human life has become a relative value. Death itself is not an evil, not even something undesirable, but a good: the entrance into Life. Death can be chosen — not the moment or manner of death, for that is the prerogative of God alone — but death, when it comes, is something man can say "Yes" to. This is not a "Yes" of resignation; not even a "Yes" of mere acceptance. It is a "Yes" of wholehearted welcome; "Father, into your hands I commend my spirit." The Christian does not simply yield to death as to the inevitable; he embraces it. Death is his most positive moment.

Now the whole meaning of Christian renunciation, as of Christian death, is that man doesn't really lose anything by either. Because he has been given God Himself as his destiny, man does not depend on any other object, person, or operation on earth in order to arrive at total human fulfillment.

He is radically free with regard to all things, because he is already in possession of All that can be his. Nothing can be taken away from him, not even life itself, that will diminish the fullness of his existence, of his life forever.

These are brave words, logical words, easy to pronounce. But to live by them is another matter — and to die by them even more difficult. When one is actually called upon to renounce values that seem essential for happiness and personal development in this world; or when at the moment of death life itself is actually slipping away, then one's faith and hope are tried like gold in the furnace, and what is only show and pretension will not hold up.

That is why Christian asceticism is called by Rahner an "exercise in Christian death".[6] To renounce real values in this world, not because circumstances require it, but freely, for the sake of *what the act of renouncing them expresses* is to "realize" our faith: to make it real, and to become aware of how really a part of our deepest selves it is. In Christian renunciation we renounce real values in this world as a way of expressing — and experiencing — that we really believe we are losing nothing thereby, that God has been given to us in grace, and that He is truly "our enough". If this act of faith has been made real in action all our life, then it will be vividly real in consolation at the moment of our death. And we will be able to affirm with confidence at that moment that God is indeed our destiny, that death itself deprives us of nothing.

Thus, in Christian renunciation what is most positive is renunciation as such, because it is the

---

[6] In "The Passion and Asceticism", p. 73 ff. and "Reflections on the Theology of Renunciation", p. 54 (in *Theological Investigations III*).

act of renunciation itself which is the expression, and the experience, of our Christian faith, hope, and love.

It follows from all we have said that Christian renunciation is by its very nature *paschal renunciation;* that is, a renunciation that is not really a loss of anything. In Christian renunciation we renounce a value that is real on one level, just to receive it back immediately on another level. We lay down our lives in order to take them up again, transformed.

This was the renunciation God asked of Abraham when He summoned him to leave "his country, his kinsfold, and his father's house" — everything that gave life its meaning here and now to a primitive, nomad tribesman — promising him in return ultimate fulfillment: the posterity without which his life's work would dissolve into nothing. For a man of Abraham's culture, individuation from the tribe was achieved by building up a herd of sheep and goats larger than the next fellow's; there was hardly any other way to distinguish oneself. But if a man died without posterity and his herd was divided up among the tribe, his life lost its distinctness, its individuality, its meaning. This was the fate childless Abraham foresaw and feared. And so God offered him a deal: the promise of ultimate meaning in life if Abraham would show faith in His promise by risking everything that gave life its meaning for him here and now. And when Abraham kept his side of the bargain — and God seemed to have kept His by giving Abraham a son, Isaac — God put Abraham to the test again, to teach him something about the full scope of the promise God had made him. Abraham thought the promise had been fulfilled: he had a son, Isaac. Isaac would have sons, and they would have sons, and Abraham would be the father of another tribe of nomads running around the desert. That was enough for Abraham. But it was not enough for God, who knew better than Abraham what man's potential was. "Take your son Isaac, whom you love, and sacrifice him to me on the mountain." In other words, Abraham was required to believe in the fulfillment of the promise while sacrificing the only possible means to its fulfillment. No question here of another son. Isaac was the child of the promise; lose him and it was finished — except that Abraham had to believe that the deal was still on.

This is the very heart and soul of an act of Christian renunciation: to sacrifice a value one understands, here on this earth, believing that one will receive back that same value, transformed into something beyond all power of understanding, in spite of the fact that there doesn't seem to be any possible way that this can be accomplished. This is faith "hoping against hope".

God gave Isaac back to Abraham transformed. He was no longer just the son who was to father another tribe of nomads to people the desert. He was to father Jesus Christ. And all who would enter into Jesus Christ through baptism, by an act of faith similar to that of Abraham — their "father in faith" — would become truly Abraham's sons: members of the Body of Christ sprung from his loins. Abraham's posterity would surpass his understanding, not just quantitatively — like the "stars of the heaven and the sands of the seashore" — but qualitatively. He would be the father of the Mystical Body of Christ.

Abraham's act of faith sets the pattern for every Christian act of faith: belief in a promise — a fulfillment, a destiny — that surpasses man's understanding; a willingness to leave everything man does understand, every visible, tangible means to fulfillment, everything on this earth that man could choose as his destiny, as an expression — a real-symbolic expression — of that belief. And faith is an act of self-determination, a disposition of one's being. It is a commitment: a commitment to "go into the land that I will show you": to follow God unreservedly, openendedly, wherever He might lead. This is the pattern of Christian death, expressed symbolically and accepted ahead of time in the sacramental sign of dying and rising again in Baptism. The real-symbolic expression of this faith-response is the whole meaning, the intrinsic value of all truly Christian asceticism, of all the acts of renunciation that take place between the Christian poles of Baptism and death, expressing the reality of the first gesture, preparing man for the reality of the last.

And so the Christian who embraces celibacy, for example, professes by this act that he does not really renounce anything he gives up! He gives up the value of spousal love on one level — the visible, tangible level of marital intercourse in this life, with all it expresses of one's love relationship with another human being — only to realize (to discover and make real) in his life, already on this earth, the truth of his spousal relationship with God through Jesus Christ. He, or she, renounces the fulfillment of biological reproduction on earth, and by this very fact enters more deeply and consciously into the mystery of the life-giving power of grace that is within us all. Christian parenthood is above all a vocation to bring children to the life of grace and raise them in the way of the Spirit. And this value, the ultimate value of biological reproduction, the religious does not renounce, becoming like Abraham, through the very faith-expression of his or her call, a "father in faith" for all of God's children, a matrix for the lifegiving seed of the word of God. In the virgin, as in the father or mother in Christian marriage, the word of God takes flesh in a particular, a specific way for the life of the world.

Through the vow of poverty, the religious renounces the pleasure and comfort of material goods,
the power and security that can be achieved through
them, and that particular means to self-development
that consists in taking responsibility, through ownership, for the management and amelioration of God's
material world. But by this same vow he affirms his
claim on the consolations and comforts of God; he
establishes himself in radical dependence on the power
and security that are found in God alone; and he
assumes an apostolic responsibility, not only toward
the poor and suffering of this world, but toward the
whole of material creation: a commitment to spend
his being in the work of reestablishing all things in
Christ. It is in fact the poor men of Christian tradition
who have sung hymns of deepest intimacy to the
beauty of this world of created things: St. Francis of
Assisi with his "Canticle of the Sun"; Father Teilhard
de Chardin with his "Hymn to the Universe". These
two examples alone would bear out the claim that
Christian poverty is a paschal renunciation: one renounces the world in order to discover the world on
a deeper level of possession.

In the vow of obedience one seems to renounce
the value of independence, of autonomous self-
direction. In fact obedience has always been presented
as a path to freedom in God. We bind ourselves to
the one who is able to take us where we want to go
but are not able. We hold out our hands so that in
the maturity of our growth another might bind us
and lead us where we would not go, yet would not
refuse to go. We do not pretend to justify the religious
tradition of vowed obedience here — that is to be
found in the treatment of the vow of obedience as
such — but only to point out that the claim of
religious obedience is that a man loses nothing of his
freedom, his self-development, or his potential to

contribute to this world by submitting himself to the government of God acting through religious superiors. The claim of religious obedience, as of all the vows, is that man loses nothing through his act of renunciation, but realizes on a higher, a transcendent level the same values he renounces on the level of ordinary human living.

What constitutes the essential, the most authentic value of the religious vows is precisely *renunciation as such* — renunciation experienced specifically as a real-symbolic expression of one's graced self responding in faith, hope, and love to the reality of Jesus Christ. It is the renunciation of tangible values on this earth — renunciation embraced for no other reason than as an act of self-expression — that gives reality, gives flesh and blood, to the expression of one's response to Jesus Christ. It is not to our point here to ask whether renunciation — in some form or other — is the *only* way to realize unambiguously the reality of a faith-response to God. But Karl Rahner poses the question very well when he claims that we cannot *really know* whether we believe in the two birds in the bush until we *let go* of the one bird in the hand.[7] It may well be that renunciation is the only authentic key to self-discovery; that this is what Jesus means when He teaches that it is only through losing our lives that we can find our lives. If risk is the authentic language of faith and hope, and self-giving the language of love, then it is easy to understand why true Christian mysticism — the realization of one's graced relationship with God — is inseparable from authentic Christian asceticism as we have explained it here.

[7] See "On the Evangelical Counsels", *Theological Investigations VIII*, p. 155.

9. *Secular life as a way of martyrdom* (See page 201 of text).

Martyrdom and monasticism have traditionally stood out as the twin peaks of Christian perfection.[8] The martyrs were the first models of total response to the Gospel. The monks of the desert succeeded them. It is my contention that we have in these models the two basic forms of all Christian spirituality: everyone who follows Christ must follow ultimately the path of the monk or the path of the martyr. All other forms of spirituality are varieties or derivations from these.

The reason for this is that Christian spirituality is by nature a spirituality of the cross. The disciple is not greater than the master. He who does not renounce everything he has, and take up his cross to follow Christ cannot be His disciple. Greater love than this no man has, that one give up his life for his friend.

And so renunciation must be a key to Christian holiness. Abnegation of self, or unselfishness, is, after all, the same reality as love: it is just the opposite side of one and the same coin. When love is real, it will express itself in the gift of self, and this will be renunciation in one form or another.

The first models Christians had of perfect renunciation in response to the Gospel were the martyrs. They were followed by the monks.

> Christians of an earlier age could look upon their heroic martyrs as the supreme models of Christian witness; for them martyrdom represented the pinnacle of Christian

---

[8] Cf. *Vatican II,* "Dogmatic Constitution on the Church," chapter 5, par. 42, (Abbott, p. 71), and chapter 7, par. 50, (Abbott, pp. 81-82).

renunciation. But since the great peace which actually preceded Constantine's conversion and especially after the conjunction of Church and State, the possibility of martyrdom had been eliminated. In the new conditions of accommodation and increasing worldliness, the holy men of the time were driven to construct a new form in which the old ideal of religion as the great renunciation might once again find expression.

(Gannon and Traub, *The Desert and the City*, Macmillan, 1969; p. 22).

This new form was religious life.

From the time of the monks of the desert until just recently; namely, until after Vatican II, it was a common assumption among Christians — among Catholics, at least — that those who "wanted to be perfect" should embrace religious life. Religious life was the way of perfection; life in the world was not.

Now, however, I think we have begun to realize that we assumed too quickly that the way of martyrdom exists only in the times of persecution. The fact of the matter is that *any* Christian living in the world, and trying to live by the Gospel, will be constantly put to the test; he will be in a constant situation of martyrdom.

This is due simply to the fact that the world as we find it is not a compatible environment for Christianity.

...The world as pluralist, secular and non-integrated is no abode of 'peace' in which man can enjoy a world that is integrated and in which the various elements are 'reconciled' and brought into harmony with one another, and one that, provided 'good will' is present, can quickly be set up. Rather it is the sphere in which man's life is one of *agon*, contest and struggle. Certainly this *agon* is directed towards a goal, namely the integration of all realities in the final fulness of the love of God as encountered 'face to face'. But this is a goal which can never fully be attained to in this age. Always it lies before us and because of this it constantly leads us into areas of fresh opportunity. But the primary demand which this *agon* makes upon us is that it shall be readily accepted — *viriliter,* as the Council of Trent expresses it. Now it is not accepted so long as man's ultimate attitude is one in which he refuses to accept and endure the pluralism of his life as non-integrated and the forces present in this life to which he is constantly exposed from the very outset.

(Karl Rahner, "Theological Reflections on the Problem of Secularisation", in *Theological Investigations X,* Herder and Herder, 1973; pp. 344-345).

In other words, religious life can be a cop-out. But religious life is not really a copping-out of the difficulties of life in this world if religious life is authentically lived. The problem comes when a Christian does not live authentically either as a religious or as a secular. For religious this usually takes the form of trying to live without real renunciation in the areas of poverty, celibacy, and obedience. For seculars it takes the form of trying to live in this world without coming into conflict with the world. But the point Rahner makes above is that conflict with this world can be sanctifying. As Christians we should expect to find ourselves in conflict with this world, and we should embrace that conflict as a means to spiritual growth. This is especially true of laypersons, of secular Christians.

The Christian simply cannot live in the world, in the sense of participating in the activities that belong to this world — business, politics, social and family life — without coming into conflict constantly with attitudes and values that are shaping his environment. The world operates by its own rules and for its own intramundane ends. Some of its principles and purposes are bad; this is the "world" in the Johannine sense, the world shaped by sin, that has hated Christ and will hate His disciples, the world to which Christ's followers do not belong. (John 15: 18-24). But some of the world's purposes and principles are not bad at all in themselves; they are just unredeemed: not formally opposed to the spirit of the Gospel, but not informed by the spirit of the Gospel either. Even the world in the good sense presents resistance to the faith-inspired idealism and world-transcending thrust of Gospel living.

All of this means that life in this world is by its very nature a struggle for graced man — and the more so the more involved he is in the activities proper to the world itself (business, politics, family and social life, etc.). More often than not, the man who tries to live uncompromisingly and whole-heartedly by the Gospel will find himself suffering persecution for his faith. It will not necessarily take the form of torture, imprisonment, or death. More often the "martyrdom" of the faithful Christian will be a simple matter of making less money in his work than is par for the profession; of losing his job again and again or being passed over for promotion; of not being acceptable to his social milieu, or not being able to accept their conversation or entertainments; of taking a stand on conscience against family, friends, or government; of not being able to make the payments on his house; of having to move out of town. None of this seems big or dramatic enough to amount to "martyrdom", but martyrdom it is. The Christian who lives in this world and plays, not by the world's rules but by the rules of Christ, can expect to lose a lot of hands. He will save his soul — his person-hood, his freedom, the integrity and final con-summation of his being — but he will do so at the price of constantly accepting to risk the loss of everything else. He who would save his life forever must live as one who is not trying to save it in this world, but rather is willing to lose it or anything that is necessary or helpful to it in this world just for the sake of bearing unblemished witness to the good news of Jesus Christ.

It may well be, of course — in fact, it is to be expected — that time and again the Christian who risks the loss of friends, possessions, or prestige will not actually lose these but even gain. God knows how to provide for His own. But we must not, from our side, set down any conditions with God. We must seek first the Kingdom of God and its justice and trust God to provide everything else that we need.

I believe that somewhere along the course of history we lost sight of the fact that the ordinary Christian life in this world is essentially a situation of martyrdom. Because we lost sight of it we grew up — and we helped others to grow up — assuming that authentic Christian life in this world was compatible with keeping a job, keeping one's friends, and doing just about everything in business, politics, and society that any other "respectable citizen" felt he had to do. As a result, whenever the ideals or principles of the Gospel appeared to us to be incompatible with normal living in this world, we concluded that we must be misunderstanding the Gospel, that it could not really mean what it seemed to mean. And so we do not invite the poor man to our table when we give a party (Luke 14: 12), we do not turn the other cheek (Matthew 5: 39), we do not take care of our neighbor as we would take care of ourselves (Matthew 7: 12), and when someone takes us to court to sue us for something we possess, we hire a lawyer and contend it (Matthew 5: 40). Christians owned slaves; segregated their schools; exploited the poor; fought in wars just and unjust alike; gave material cooperation to tyrannical or totalitarian governments; bought and sold, ate, and dressed, and drank like the children of this world, and went to Communion regularly every Sunday. Christians still do these things and still go to Communion every Sunday, not conscious of a problem.

As long as it was taken for granted that Christians living in the world had to be "realistic" in their accommodation to the attitudes and practices of their cultural milieu (and "being realistic" meant following the slogan that says, "When you can't lick 'em, join 'em"), it was natural that religious life — that is, simply "leaving" the world — would appear to be the only uncompromising form of evangelical living. How can a man realistically follow the Gospel if he has to make a living, has to deal with non-believers in a pluralistic society, mix in their social gatherings, participate in the business and political decisions of his cultural milieu? He can do this, and maintain his integrity as a Christian, only if he is prepared to consider it normal that he should risk everything he has every day of his life. This is a spirituality of martyrdom. But Christians assumed that the first premiss in any moral decision was *primum est vivere*: first you survive. To bear Christian witness in business you first had to stay in business. To be a leaven for good in society, you first had to keep your position in society. To provide Catholic education for the young you first had to preserve your schools. And so Christians did not take a stand on social justice, on segregation, on compromising business and political practices.

We were taught that it was permissible to give material cooperation to evil projects provided that the evil would go on without our cooperation anyway, and that if we refused our cooperation we would suffer a proportionately serious evil ourselves. So we accommodated, we "went along" with the evil of this world so long as we were not asked to do the formally, the explicitly evil thing ourselves. We could not pull the trigger, but we could provide the gun. We would not be personally cruel to black people ourselves, but we would conduct schools in a segregated system. The point of St. Thomas More's example was lost on us: we thought we could contribute as Christians to life in the city of man and not expect death as our wages.

St. Thomas More felt called to religious life. He tried the Carthusians. But God showed him that it was not religious life as such he was called to, but simply the perfection of the Gospel. So he returned to the city of man, became Chancellor of the Realm, and died on the executioner's block.

Joan of Arc paid the same entrance fee for her contribution as a lay Christian to the secular life of her times.

It is not my purpose here to prove the hypothesis that secular spirituality is essentially a spirituality of martyrdom. This is a book on religious life, not on lay spirituality.[9] I only want to establish in some credible way that seculars are called along the path of renunciation, the path of the cross, no less than religious. The difference is that seculars live in this world and risk all they have, while religious give up the benefits of life in this world to begin with and have little left to risk. But the underlying reality of both spiritualities is the way of the cross.

The conclusion to be drawn from this is very simple, but it doesn't appear to be widely understood. The conclusion is that religious should follow the path of renunciation as such, and laypersons should follow the path of risk. Religious should concentrate on being really poor, really celibate (with all the

[9] I have a book on lay spirituality that will appear soon under the title *Is The Good News Really News,* St. Anthony Messenger Press, Cincinnati, Ohio.

positive commitments that implies), really surrendered in obedience. Laypersons should concentrate on uncompromising witness to the Gospel in an unreceptive or hostile world and expect to be crucified for their stance.

Both laypersons and religious will participate a great deal, of course, in the spirituality of one another. Christian spiritualities overlap; there is not much in the Gospel that any group can claim to have a monopoly on. But if religious and laypersons can both recognize the characteristic currents of their own spirituality, they will better know how to accept and use the thrust of those currents to arrive at the perfection of charity.

"DONUM DEI" SERIES

1. *Religious Holiness and Apostolic Life,* 104 pp.
   F. Jetté, N. Morissette   **$1.00**

2. *Religious Poverty in the Modern World,* 131 pp.
   Mgr S. Baggio, Mgr M. J. Lemieux, J. E. MacGuigan,
   C. M. Matura, P. M. Poisson, A. J. Thomas.   **$1.00**

3. *Religious Obedience and the Exercise of Authority,* 209 pp.
   M. Bélanger, L. J. Bondy, G. George, J. Laplace, R.
   Morency, R. Cardinal Villeneuve.   **$1.25**

4. *The States of Perfection in Their Ecclesial Perspective,*
   124 pp.
   Y. Charron, R. Lechner, F. Smith, J. M. R. Tillard,
   V. Cardinal Valeri.   *(Out of print.)*

5. *On the Eve of the Second Vatican Council,* 68 pp.
   His Holiness, John XXIII, Mgr S. Baggio, J. Rous-
   seau.   *(Out of print.)*

6. *Religious Chastity: Its Conditions,* 245 pp.
   W. C. Bier, G. Kelly, J. Laplace, A. M. Perreault,
   A. Plé.   **$1.65**

7. *Serving the Church in Latin America,* 188 pp.
   His Holiness, Pius XII, His Holiness, John XXIII,
   Mgr A. Casaroli, F. Houtart.   **$1.00**

8. *Liturgy and Religious Life,* 208 pp.
   Mgr S. Baggio, M. Chamberlain, M. Dubois, L. J.
   Fischer, A. Legault, Mgr A. Martin, Mgr P. Phi-
   lippe.   *(Out of print.)*

9. *Principles for a Renewal of Religious Life,* 102 pp.
   Mgr P. Philippe, J. F. Barbier, J. Hamer.   **$0.75**

10. *Religious and Dialogue with the World,* 252 pp.
    His Holiness, Paul VI, Mgr G. B. Flahiff, J. Gervais,
    F. Houtart, D. M. Huot, A. F. Mackenzie, J. M. R.
    Tillard, R. Voillaume.   **$1.75**

"VITA EVANGELICA" SERIES

(Kindly add thirty cents per volume for mailing charges.)

PUBLICATIONS OF THE CANADIAN
RELIGIOUS CONFERENCE
324 Laurier Avenue East
Ottawa, Ont., Canada
K1N 6P6

14539   IMPRIMERIE NOTRE-DAME INC.